More Chess and Computers

The Microcomputer Revolution
The Challenge Match

COMPUTER CHESS SERIES

More Chess and Computers

The Microcomputer Revolution
The Challenge Match

David Levy
Monroe Newborn

Computer Science Press

© Copyright 1980 Computer Science Press, Inc.

Printed in the United States of America

Published simultaneously in the United States of America and Great Britian by:

Computer Science Press, Inc.
9125 Fall River Lane
Potomac, Maryland 20854 U.S.A.

B. T. Batsford Ltd.
4 Fitzhardinge Street
London W1H OAH
Great Britain

1 2 3 4 5   84 83 82 81 80

Library of Congress Cataloging in Publication Data

Levy, David N   L
   More chess and computers.

   (Computer chess books)
   Bibliography: p.
   1. Chess—Data processing.   2. Chess—Tournaments.
3. Microcomputers.   I. Newborn, Monroe, joint author.
II. Title.   III. Series.
GV1318.L483   1980   794.1′7   80-16057
ISBN 0-914894-07-2
UK ISBN   0   7134   2692   6

To Lily and Floyd and the memory of Pumpernickel.

"A fool sees not the same tree that a wise man sees."

William Blake

Contents

Preface

This is my fourth work for Computer Science Press, Inc., who have done much to help the advancement of computer chess by publishing regularly on the subject. The present volume was written in cooperation with Monty Newborn. Chapter 5 is his exclusive contribution. In addition, he assisted in coordinating material. This book is intended to be a sequel to *Chess and Computers,* and to bring the reader of that work up to date on developments that have taken place in the field during the past three years. However, it is by no means essential for those interested in the subject to have read the earlier work before they can follow the present one - simply consider *More Chess and Computers* as a state of the art survey.

Perhaps I should devote a few words to the future of this series of books on computer chess. I will not be writing any more tournament books but will condense the results and games of the most important computer chess tournaments into a succession of books which will appear at three yearly intervals, following the triennial IFIP Congress at which the World Computer Championship is held. The next volume in this series may therefore be expected after the 1980 IFIP Congress which is due to take place in Melbourne.

Computer Chess is a discipline which is attracting widespread interest from scientists and from the chess playing public. At the present time there is considerably less literature being published on the subject than on human chess. Within a decade or so I expect this situation to change dramatically - as computer programs begin to become regular winners of Grandmaster tournaments there is no reason why they cannot be used to annotate games in chess periodicals and to 'write' articles on new ideas in the openings. It would not surprise me at all if, within a decade, there were at least half a dozen monthly magazines devoted largely or exclusively to the latest games and exploits of computer programs. Ten years ago I would not have believed possible the progress that has since been made. Now nothing would really surprise me (very much).

David Levy
London, June 1979

1 The Levy Bet - End of an Era

In August 1968—I attended a conference on Artificial Intelligence at Edinburgh University's Department of Machine Intelligence and Perception. At a cocktail party one evening during the conference, I happened to be playing a friendly game of chess with John McCarthy, a professor of Artificial Intelligence at Stanford University and one of the world's leading authorities in his field. I won the game, and he remarked that although he was not strong enough for me, he thought that within ten years there would be a computer program that could beat me. You can imagine my reaction. I was the reigning Scottish Chess Champion at the time, and here was this inexpert player telling me that in only a few years I would succumb to a computer program! I said something roughly equivalent to (but more polite than) "put your money where your mouth is," and I offered to bet Professor McCarthy £500 (then worth $1,250) that he was wrong. Our host for the evening, Professor Donald Michie, who was sitting on the floor only a couple of feet away, joined in our debate and agreed to take half of the bet, McCarthy taking the other half.

A year later I returned to Edinburgh to deliver a paper at the Machine Intelligence Workshop. In the audience was Professor Seymour Papert of the Massachusettes Institute of Technology. He was so sure I was wrong that he wanted to take the bet for a five-year period, but I wouldn't let him. He therefore joined the original duet, adding £250 to the bet.

In 1971, a fourth member of the consortium was added: Professor Ed Kozdrowicki of the University of California at Davis wanted to bet me $1,000 that I was wrong, and at that time the bet had only seven years to run. A thousand dollars seemed like an awful lot of money to me at that time—I was suffering the usual impecuniousness of the chess master—so I took only £250 of the action ($650), and my friend Ben Mittman, who runs the computer center at Northwestern University, took the rest of Professor Kozdrowicki's bet. (Later that same day Kozdrowicki's program, COKO III, failed to play a mate in one, then failed again, and again—and finally lost! Ed rushed out of the room mumbling something about a bad bet . . .)

That is how things stood for four years. Then, in the winter of 1975, Donald Michie made me an offer I couldn't refuse. He wanted to increase his original £250 bet to £500 and to add a further £500 bet that if I did lose it would be a program developed by him or under his guidance. I accepted both bets without hesitation, feeling that the second bet gave me a kind of insurance policy: if I was going to lose the original bet it would almost certainly be to the Northwestern program or to Russia's KAISSA.

My original bet was now up to £1,250 (now worth only $2,500) because of the sinking value of the pound Sterling), and that is where it finished.

The Challenges

Until 1977 there seemed to be no point in my playing a formal challenge match against any chess program simply because none of them were good enough. But when CHESS 4.5, written by David Slate and Larry Atkin, began to do well in human events (winning the 1977 Minnesota Open, for a rather remarkable example), it was time for me to face up to my responsibilities and to defend the human race against the coming invasion.

My first match was arranged by Donald Michie, who was then a visitor at Carnegie-Mellon University in Pittsburgh. The conditions of the match were that I would play two games, but that if I won the first game the match would be over since it would then be impossible for the program to score the $1\frac{1}{2}$ points required to beat me. The game was played on April 1st under really excellent playing conditions. I was seated in a closed room with a T.V. camera, a video display unit, and one or both of CHESS 4.5's programmers. The camera was linked to a television set in an auditorium where perhaps 400 people watched the game at one time or another. Hans Berliner commented on the game throughout, and when it was over I went into the auditorium to say a few words about how I felt while I was playing the game. I must say that those responsible for organising the match in Pittsburgh did a wonderful job and I have never participated in an event where the players were more comfortable. The organisors even arranged for the moves of the game to be transmitted over the ARPA satellite network so that hundreds of people were able to follow the course of the game (including McCarthy at Standford and Papert at M.I.T.).

I won the toss and chose Black in the first game. This choice of colour was decided by the fact that in the eight blitz games that I had played against the program a few days earlier, I had repeatedly got very good positions from the opening with my favourite Dragon variation as Black, but had only been able to get slight advantages with White. The night before I played the game I went along to inspect the playing conditions but was asked to leave the playing room because Berliner was modifying the program's opening book. I happened to wander into the auditorium where I noticed the printer that was to be used to keep the audience up to date with the progress in my game, and as I glanced down I saw that the printing head was moving. So there I stood, watching the printer, as Berliner did his best to bolster up the program's knowledge of the Dragon Variation!

White: CHESS 4.5
Black: Levy

Pittsburgh, April 1st 1977
Sicilian Defence

1	P-K4	P-QB4
2	N-KB3	P-Q3
3	P-Q4	P×P
4	N×P	N-KB3
5	N-QB3	P-KN3
6	P-B3	B-N2
7	B-K3	O-O
8	Q-Q2	N-B3
9	B-QB4	

In a couple of blitz games the program had played 9 0-0-0 against me and I had replied 9...P-QR3 to take the program out of its book. It then played 10 NxN?! and after 10...P×N I won both games with a direct assault down the QN-file. Berliner's changes were designed to improve the program's play from move 9 onwards but instead of playing 9...B-Q2, the move which he had prepared the previous evening, I thought that once again I would try to trick the program.

9 ... P-QR3

Against a human player I would give this move a question mark because it is too slow. Against this program it deserves an exclamation point because when the program does not know what to do against the Sicilian it captures on QB6.

10 N×N?!

There are two reasons why the program' made this move. Firstly, my QB3 knight attacks two central squares and so in a sense it appears to be more valuable than White's

Q4 knight. Also, all programs know that isolated pawns are weak and my QRP now becomes isolated. Since the text strengthens my pawn centre I was quite happy.

10 ... P × N

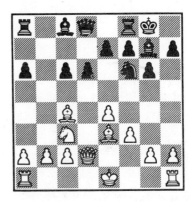

11 0-0 N-Q2

Against a human I would never transfer this knight from the king side, where it is needed for defence, to the queen side, but I knew that CHESS 4.5 does not know how to mount a K-side attack.

12 P-B4 N-N3
13 B-K2 B-K3

Intending ...N-B5.

14 P-QN3?

The move I expected and a mistake, 14 B-Q4 is correct, but programs are quite prone to making weakening pawn moves because they have little understanding of strong and weak squares.

14 ... N-B1

Continuing my policy of doing nothing, or very little, apart from encouraging the program to weaken its position.

15   P-QR3
Intending to meet ...Q-R4 with P-QN4, but 15 B-Q4 was still correct.

15   ...   Q-R4
Encouraging another pawn advance.

16   P-QN4
Thank you!

16   ...   Q-B2

17   P-B5
Now White's K5 square is weak and his KP is in some danger of becoming isolated.

17   ...   B-Q2

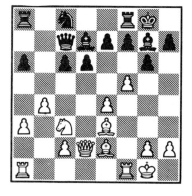

18   B-R6
The right idea but the wrong way to set about it. The correct plan begins with 18 K-R1, followed by R-B3, B-R6 and R-R3. It is easy for a human to find such a plan but not for a computer program. CHESS 4.5 was looking roughly six half-moves deep along every single variation and then examining checks and captures at deeper levels. While this process enables it to see 25 half-moves or more along tactical paths, it does not allow it to examine the seven half-move continuation beginning with 18 K-R1 simply because White's moves are all "quiet" moves, i.e. not captures or checks.

Now the reader will understand why I was not afraid to move my knight at move eleven. I was absolutely confident that the program would not have the conceptual ability to mount such an attack. In the auditorium however, Hans Berliner was telling the audience that the program had the advantage at this stage (before B-R6) - a statement which may have been true in a human v human game but which was certainly not true in a computer program v human encounter.

18   ...   Q-N3ch
19   K-R1   Q-Q5!
It is this manoeuvre which refutes White's 18th move. The exchange of queens leads to an ending in which the weaknesses in the program's pawn structure must ultimately prove fatal.

20   Q × Q   B × Q
21   R-B3
If 21 B × R B × N 22 B-R6 B × R 23 R × B P × P 24 P × P B × P, winning a pawn. CHESS 4.5 would certainly have seen this variation and rejected it.

21   ...   B-N2
22   B × B   K × B
23   R-QN1   N-N3
24   R(3)-B1
Aimless play. In this type of position it is essential to have some sort of plan.

24   ...   KR-QN1
25   QR-Q1   P-B3

Possibly not necessary, but I wanted to avoid any tactical possibilities at a later stage which might involve P-K5 or P-B6ch by White.

28	...	R-QB1
29	R-Q3	R-B4
30	R-N3	R(1)-QB1
31	R(1)-B3	P-R5
32	P-R4	

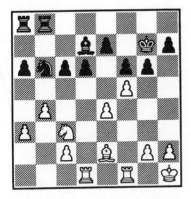

26 P-QR4?

This move was based on the analysis of 419,165 positions and a look-ahead which extended to 22 half-moves. The program thought at this point that it had an advantage equivalent to roughly half a pawn, but in fact the text makes the win very easy for Black. Were it not for this move, or some other equally weak response from the program, it would have taken many moves to exploit White's weaknesses.

26	...	P-QR4
27	P-N5	BP×P
28	RP×P	

28 B×P B×B P×B R-QB1 would not be very much different from the game continuation. Now White thought that it was seven-eighths of a pawn ahead!

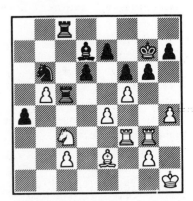

CHESS 4.5 still thought that it was ahead (by half a pawn).

32	....	P-R6
33	P×P	

But now it realized that the truth was somewhat different and it printed out an evaluation of three-quarters of a pawn in Black's favour.

33	...	P×P
34	R-K3	B-K3
35	P-R5	P-N4
36	N-Q5	P-R7
37	R-QR3	B×N
38	P×B	R×BP
39	B-Q1	R-Q7
40	K-R2	R-B8
41	B-N3	P-R8=Q
42	R×Q	R×R
43	R-K3	

At this point the programmers decided to **resign** for their program.

After this game David Slate and Larry Atkin said that they thought it unlikely that they would challenge me again until August 1978 because they realized that their program needed a substantial improvement before it would have a chance of victory. But CHESS 4.5 is not the only strong program in the world. Since KAISSA had finished first at the 1974 World Computer Championships, Donald Michie, who had taken the role of leader of the consortium who had bet against me, thought that a match between myself and KAISSA would be worthwhile, particularly in view of the fact that at the second World Championship in Toronto, KAISSA would be running on an IBM machine, rather than the slower ICL computer used in 1974, and there was the additional possibility that an Amdahl computer might be available. A match was set up for Toronto, a few days after the end of the World Championship, but it proved impossible to get the program working on an Amdahl computer in time for the match. A postponement of a few days was agreed, and I set up a board and clock in my motel room in Columbus, Ohio, from where I was communicating with Toronto by telephone and Donald Michie waited anxiously for something to happen on the Amdahl 470 V/6 in Sunnyvale, California. Again nothing happened. Finally, after a 29 hour journey that involved a sandstorm and a broken aircraft engine, I arrived in Montreal one cold afternoon in December 1977 to play against KAISSA from a room at McGill University. The match had been set up by Monty Newborn and this time all systems at Sunnyvale were 'go'. As at Pittsburgh, this was scheduled as a two game match, and once again I won the toss. This time I chose white. It should be mentioned on behalf of Donsky and Arlazarv that the group at Sunnyvale were very green at managing KAISSA. Newborn feels they didn't know how to take full advantage of the Amdahl and consequently KAISSA was probably below top form.

White: Levy
Black: KAISSA

Montreal, December 17th 1977
English Opening (by transposition)

1   P-Q3

This move was designed to take KAISSA out of its openings book and to avoid an early clash of forces. I was following my dictum of doing nothing but doing it well, and waiting for the program to dig its own grave.

	1 ...	N-QB3
2	P-QB4	P-K4
3	P-KN3	B-B4

Already an inaccurate move. The bishop has no real future on the QR2-KN8 diagonal since White can blunt its attack by P-K3.

4	B-N2	N-B3
5	N-QB3	0-0
6	P-K3	Q-K2

A pointless move that puts the queen on a bad square.

7	KN-K2	B-N3
8	0-0	P-Q3
9	P-QR3	B-N5

9 ...P-QR4 was necessary, to prevent White's next move.

| 10 | P-QN4 | Q-K3 |
| 11 | N-Q5 | B×N |

I was pleased when KAISSA made this move but could not understand why it should do so. Black's bishop is undoubtedly a better piece than my knight.

12	Q×B	N-N5

13 B-Q2

I also considered 13 B-R3 P-B4 14 P-K4, but rejected it as being unnecessarily sharp.

13	...	QR-N1

I was threatening 14 P-B5! P×P 15 P×P B-R4 (or 15 ...B×P 16 N×P) 16 B×B N×B 17 N×P, forking Black's queen and rook.

14	P-QR4	P-QR3

Relatively best was 14 ...P-QR4 15 P-N5 N-Q1 16 N×B P×N, though White can then win a pawn by 17 B-R3 P-B4 18 P-K4 N-R3 19 B×N Q×B 20 B×BP.

15	P-R5	B-R2
16	P-N5	P×P
17	P×P	P-K5!

The best swindling try. If now 18 P×N Q×N 19 B×P, Black replies 19...Q-R4, saving the piece. Best was 18 P×P N(B3)-K4 19 P-N6, but who makes the best moves after a 29

hour journey? In any case, the move that I chose was quite sufficient.

18	P×N	Q×N
19	Q×N	Q×QP
20	KR-Q1	P-B4
21	Q-N5	P×P
22	B-KB1	Q-N6
23	R(Q1)-B1	P-R3
24	Q-N6	

24	...	Q-N2

Forced. Black must guard against 25 R×P and 25 B-B4ch forking king and queen. If 24...R-B3 25 Q×R! P×Q 26 B-B4ch Q×B 27 R×Q.

25	P-R6	Q-B1

On 25...Q-R1 I had planned 26 B-B4ch, and if 26...P-Q4 27 B×Pch! P×B 28 R×P and mate on KN7.

26	R×P	R-B3
27	Q-R5	Q-Q2
28	R(R1)-B1	B-B4
29	R(B1)×B!	P×R
30	R×R	P×R

Black's 28th move was designed to win material, but in doing so Black left its king fatally exposed. Programs still seem to be unable to judge when material is not the most important feature in a position.

31	Q-N6ch	Q-N2
32	Q × P(B5)	

At this point the game was adjudicated by Camille Coudari, a Canadian Intentional Master. White has a material advantage and numerous threats, as a result of which Black is totally lost. e.g.: (a) 33 P-R7 R-R1 34 Q-Q5ch, winning the rook; (b) 33 B-B4ch K-R1 34 B-B3 R-KB1 35 P-R7 and then 36 P-R8 = Q R × Q 37 B × P winning the queen; (c) 33 Q × KP, threatening 34 P-R7 etc.

Coudari therefore adjudicated the game a *win for White*.

With the bet having only several months to run, Slate began devoting half of his working time to a new program, a complete rewirte that would be named CHESS 5.0. I had decided some time ago that I wanted to play my final match in a blaze of publicity (the deadline was the end of August 1978), and I had tried to persuade the Canadian National Exhibition to sponsor it. After various difficulties the match was finally scheduled at CNE.

About three weeks before leaving England for Toronto, I received a most unexpected challenge from Richard Greenblatt of M.I.T. Greenblatt, it will be recalled, was the author of the program **MACHACK VI,** which achieved fame around 1957 by finding a pretty Rook sacrifice that had been overlooked by a number of U.S. masters. Although very little news of chess had been emanating from M.I.T.'s Artificial Intelligence labs during the past decade, scientists there were known to be working on a piece of hardware designed to do nothing but analyze, generate, and evaluate chess positions at the rate of 150,000 per second!! This machine, called CHEOPS, would be used by an improved version of the Greenblatt program in the following way: whenever the main program reached a position it considered strategically satisfactory, CHEOPS would take a look at the further tactical possibilities. This enabled the program to avoid numerous traps.

I agreed to a two-game match against the Greenblatt **MACHACK-CHEOPS** program. Since I had wagered that I would not lose a match, I needed to score only one point in the two games. The rate of play for all my challenge matches had been agreed at forty moves in two hours followed by twenty moves per hour. Under these conditions the following game was played in Cambridge, Massachusetts, on August 23, 1978.

White: MACHACK
Black: Levy

Sicilian Defence

1	P-K4	P-QB4

Since I knew nothing about this program's style or openings repertoire, I thought it best to play something with which I was reasonably familiar rather than try to confuse the program from the outset.

2	N-KB3	P-Q3
3	P-Q4	P × P

4 N×P   N-KB3
5 N-QB3   P-KN3
6 P-B4

I began to smell a rat. I knew that U.S. international masters Ken Rogoff and Norman Weinstein had visited M.I.T. a few days earlier, and I was worried that one of them might have busted a line in my book on the Dragon Sicilian. But now it was too late to turn back.

6 ...   B-N2!

This move, which used to be considered a grave error, is probably Black's best reply.

7 P-K5   N-R4
8 B-N5 ch

Not 8 P-KN4?? N×P B×N P×P winning a pawn.

8 ...   B-Q2
9 P-K6   P×P
10 N×P   B×N ch
11 P×B

Thus far both sides have been following a well-known path which used to be thought very good for White.

11 ...   Q-B1!

A relatively new idea, maintaining threats against QB6, QN4, and K3, which I think rehabilitates 6 ...B-N2. During the game, however, I could not help worrying that the program was about to unleash a crushing innovation, courtesy of Rogoff or Weinstein. All of **MAC HACK's** moves thus far had been played without hesitation. But now it "thought" for a couple of minutes, so I knew that my earlier fears were unfounded. I learned later that the opening book had been prepared by Ken Church, one of Greenblatt's research students, and he had not even used my book!

12 Q-Q4   N-KB3
13 Q-B4   N-B3
14 N-Q4   N×N

Exchanging into a slightly favourable end-game.

15 P×N

If 15 B×B ch Q×B 16 P×N (or 16 Q×N Q-K3 ch and White's King is the more exposed) 16 ...R-QB1 with a good game for Black.

15 ...   Q×Q
16 B×Q   B-B4!

More accurate than 16 ...R-QB1 17 B-Q3 when it is not clear that Black has any advantage.

17 B-N5 ch

To stop me from castling; not that I would want to.

17 ...   K-B2
18 B-B4 ch   P-Q4
19 B-Q3!

Excellent judgement. After 19 B-N3 the bishop would be badly placed and Black would pile up on the QB-pawn without worrying about counterplay along the QN-file. Black can capture on Q3 at once, saddling White with doubled, isolated pawns, but in fact this would leave Black's knight without a really good square.

19	...	KR-QB1
20	0-0	

I was told after the game that the strategic part of the program wanted to trade bishops on KB5, but CHE-OPS realized that this would leave the QB-pawn indefensible. When the program castled, the audience, who had been following this thought process, let out a cheer. I was happy because the text move shows that the program did not understand what was going to happen. The King is needed in the middle to protect the QB2/Q3 structure.

20	...	R-B2
21	R-N1	QR-QB1
22	B-K3?!	N-K5
23	R-B3	

White's rather aimless play here-abouts is reminiscent of the way CHESS 4.6 played against me in Pittsburgh.

23	...	N-Q3
24	R-N2	P-N3

25	P-QR4	B × B

Now that my pieces are on their best square and the QN-pawn is protected it is time to cash in on the weaknesses of White's pawn structure.

26	P × B	R-B6
27	R-R3	P-KR4
28	B-Q2	R-B7
29	R × R	R × R
30	B-K1	N-B4
31	P-R5	P × P
32	B × P	N × P
33	R-K3	R-R7
34	B-B7	P-R4

Outside passed pawns seem awfully strong against chess programs (CHESS 4.6 v. Levy, *Chess Life and Review,* June 1977).

35	R-K1	P-QR5
36	B-K5	N-B3
37	B-R8	P-R6
38	R-Q1	R-QB7
39	B-R1	P-R7
40	P-R3	N-R4
41	P-Q4	N-N6
42	P-B5	R-B8
43	R × R	

Greenblatt resigned for his program because of 43 ...N × R, 44 ...N-N6, etc.

Greenblatt asked me to play the second game at 30-30 speed, and I agreed. It was a dull game, in which I outplayed the program in a Rook ending only to reach a position in which my extra pawn might not have been enough to win against best play, but **MACHACK,** after very cleverly seeing a number of tricks, went completely wrong and lost.

The Main Event

The final match to decide the bet began on August 26 at the Canadian National Exhibition in Toronto. CHESS 5.0 was not ready in time, so I played its predecessor, CHESS 4.7. I was seated in an almost soundproof booth, wearing a tuxedo. The program was represented by David Slate (his partner was vacationing in England), David Cahlander, and John Douglas, the latter two of Control Data Corporation. Cahlander had built a special chessboard with a switch beneath each square to enable the program to detect its opponents' moves. The switches are activated by magnets in the bases of the chess pieces. This board also indicates the program's moves automatically, by lighting up the departure and arrival squares as well as the other squares along the moving piece's path. Soon a robot will move the pieces for the program and punch the clock button.

The Toronto match was scheduled for six games. I therefore needed three points to collect my wager; my opponent needed three and a half to make me famous.

The notes to the five games of the Toronto match are by CHESS 4.7 and myself. The first line of each note contains four items of information: (1) The program's assessment of its position, expressed in pawns (thus, after 3...N-KB3 in game 1, CHESS 4.7 considered itself to be 0.13 of a pawn behind); (2) In parentheses, the number of positions evaluated when considering this move; the number of seconds taken by the program over its move; and the number of iterations performed by the program's search process (this is the depth, in ply, of the exhaustive part of the search).

The second line of annotation is the program's predicted continuation, i.e., its opinion of the best line of play for both sides.

In some positions I have added a note of my own, and this always follows the program's comments.

GAME 1
White: Levy
Black: CHESS 4.7
Reversed Pirc

1	P-KN3	P-Q4 (book)
2	B-N2	P-K4 (book)
3	P-Q3	N-KB3

-0.13 (230,531; 76; 6)
4 N-QB3 B-QB4 5 N-R4 N-R3 6 B-Q2

| 4 | N-KB3 | N-B3 |

-0.15 (208,660; 69; 6)
5 P-Q4 P×P 6 N×P B-N5 7 N×N P×N

| 5 | 0-0 | B-Q2 |

-0.13 (339,183; 118; 6)
6 B-Q2 B-QB4

| 6 | P-N3 | B-QB4 |

-0.20 (281,184; 96; 6)
7 N-B3 P-Q5 8 N-QR4 B-QN5 9 N-N5

| 7 | B-N2 | Q-K2 |

-0.26 (384,803; 129; 6)
8 N-B3 0-0 9 N-QN5

| 8 | P-QR3 | P-K5 |

-0.43 (346,157; 116; 6)
9 P×P P×P 10 KN-Q2 0-0 11 N×P N×N 12 B×N Q×B 13 Q×B Q×BP

| 9 | N-K1 | 0-0 |

-0.54 (557,445; 195; 6)
10 P×P P×P 11 P-QN4 B-N3 12 N-Q2

| 10 | P-Q4 | B-Q3 |

-0.56 (207,493; 67; 6)
11 N-QB3 P-QR3 12 P-B4 K-R1

11   P-K3

Before you all rush off letters complaining about my opening play, permit me to point out that when faced with a strong computer program I try to play the opponent, not the position. It was my plan to create a situation in which nothing was happening and then to expand gradually on the Queenside. Unfortunately, the program had read my article in the June 1977 *Chess Life and Review* and found out how to attack on the Kingside.

11   ...   N-KN5!

-0.55 (677,730; 264; 6)

12 P-R3 N-B3 13 N-QB3 P-QR3 14 P-B4

12   P-R3??

12 P-QB4 must be played but even then 12 ...Q-N4 is strong. I completely overlooked Black's 13th move.

12   ...   N × KP!!

-0.62 (1,508,192; 509; 8)

13 P × N Q-N4 14 Q-K2 Q × P 15 N-QB3 Q-R7 ch 16 K-B2

The program replied instantly, indicating that it had expected 12 P-R3 and had already worked out its reply while I was thinking!

13   P × N   Q-N4

-0.62 (189,389; 66; 6)

14 Q-K2 Q × P 15 N-QB3 Q-R7 ch 16 K-B2

14   P-KN4

Realizing that I was completely busted, I thought my only hope was to sacrifice the Exchange to get the queens off.

14   ...   Q × P ch

-1.43 (196,923; 67; 6)

15 K-R1 Q-N6 16 K-N1 Q-R7 ch 17 K-B2

15   R-B2   B-N6

-2.31 (264,087; 78; 6)

16 Q-Q2 B × R ch 17 Q × R Q × Q ch 18 K × Q

16   Q-K2   Q × R ch

-2.47 (328,495; 89, 7)

17 Q × Q B × Q ch 18 K × Q P-B4 19 P × P B × P

Of course it would be crushing to take with the bishop and keep the queens on so that my king would die of exposure, but the program knows that it should trade down when materially ahead.

17   Q × Q   B × Q ch

-2.47 (325,505; 85; 8)

18 K × Q P-B4 19 P × P

18   K × B   P-B4!

-2.45 (275,094; 80; 7)

19 P × P B × P 20 K-K3 B-Q2 21 N-Q2 QR-K1

19   P × P   N-K2

-2.46 (419,456; 125; 7)

20 K-N1 N × P 21 N-QB3 B-B3 22 R-B1 N-K6

20   P-B4   R × P ch

-2.34 (292,433; 84; 7)

21 K-N1 P-B3 22 B-QB1 QR-KB1 23 B-K3 R/4-B3

21   K-N1   P-B3

-2.23 (504,277; 153; 7)

22 P-QR4 N-N3 23 N-QB3 N-R5 24 B-R3 R-K1

22   N-QB3   R-R4

-2.24 (1,024,267; 315; 7)

23 N-K2 N-N3 24 K-R2 N-R5 25 N-N3 R-N4

23   K-R2   R-KB1

-2.20 (586,076; 177; 7)

24 B-QB1 N-B4 25 P × P P × P 26

N × QP N × P

24 N-Q1   **N-N3**

-2.67 (560,787; 167; 7)

25 R-B1 N-B5 26 R-B3 P × P 27 B × P P × P 28 R × P R × P ch 29 R × R B × R

25 R-B1   **B × P!**

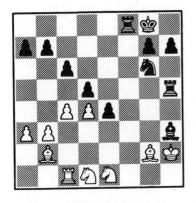

-3.11 (574,126; 166; 7)

26 B × B R-B8 27 N-K3 R-B7 ch 28 N-N2 R × N ch

I had seen this coming but was powerless to prevent it.

26 B × B   **R-B8**

-2.53 (1,091,773; 279; 8)

27 N-K3 R-B7 ch 28 K-N1 R × B 29 B-K6 ch K-R1 30 P × P R × NP 31 P × P R × N 32 P × P

27 N-N2   **R-B6**

-3.33 (956,766; 239; 8)

28 K-N1 R/4 × B 29 P × P P × P 30 R-B5 N-K2 31 R-B7

28 P × P   **R/4 × B ch**

-3.22 (1,030,153; 245; 8)

29 K-N1 P × P 30 R-B5 N-K2 31 R-B7 N-B3 32 N-B2

29 K-N1   **P × P**

-3.20 (338,469; 94; 8)

30 R-B8 ch R-B1 31 R × R ch

K × R 32 N/1-K3 N-K2 33 K-B2

30 R-B8 ch   **N-B1?**

-3.06 (1,293,137; 366; 9)

31 N-B3 R-Q6 32 N-B4 R/Q-N6 ch 33 N-N2 R-N4 34 R-B7 R/6-N6

31 B-B3   **R-Q6**

-4.71 (578,439; 145; 8)

32 N/1-K3 R/R × N 33 N × R R × N 34 K-B2 R-B6 ch 35 K-K2

32 N/1-K3   **R/R × N**

-4.74 (462,088; 121; 9)

33 N × R R × N 34 B-N4 R-N6 ch 35 K-B2

33 N × R   **R × N**

-3.55 (516,744; 135; 9)

34 B-N4 R-KB6 35 R-Q8

34 B-N4

My first threat of the game, but I was not too happy about being three pawns down.

34 ...   **R-KB6**

-3.47 (487,332; 137; 8)

35 R-Q8 P-KR3 36 B × N R × B 37 R × P P-KN4 38 R-Q7

35 R-Q8   **P-KR3**

-3.47 (708,097; 195; 8)

36 B × N R × B 37 R × P P-KN4 38 R-K5 R-B5 39 R-K7

The program no doubt saw that 35 ... R-B4 36 B × N R × B 37 R × P would be followed by the win of the K-pawn or the QN-pawn and probably did not analyse past that point.

36 R × P   **R × P**

-4.30 (758,637; 202; 8)

37 R-QR5 P-R3 38 R-K5 P-K6 39 R-K7 R-Q6 40 K-N2 R × QP 41 R × KP

37 R-Q8   **R-KB6**

-3.12 (1,682,751; 473; 9)

38 R-K8 R-B5 39 K-N2 P-KN4 40

P-Q5 P-KR4 41 B×N R×B 42
R×P

38   R-R8   P-KN4

-3.32 (732,704; 204; 8)

39 R-K8 P-K6 40 P-Q5 P-KR4 41
B×N R×B 42 R×P

39   P-Q5   P-KR4

-3.25 (571,760; 159; 8)

40 R×P R-B4 41 R-R8 K-N2 42
R-K8 N-R2 43 R×P R×P

40   P-Q6   K-N2

-3.31 (501,877; 138; 8)

41 R×P R-B2 42 B-B3 ch K-N3

41   R×P   R-B2

-2.47 (677,184; 182; 9)

42 R-R5 K-N3 43 R-K5 R-B5 44
R-N5 P-N3 45 R×P N-Q2

42   R-R5

Suddenly the position is no longer
totally hopeless - it is merely
hopeless.

42   ...   K-B3

-2.24 (1,312,720; 363; 9)

43 K-B2 P-N3 44 R-N5 K-K3 45
K-K3 R-B4 46 R×P N-Q2

43   B-B3 ch   K-N3

-2.53 (667,411; 183; 9)

44 R-K5 R-B5 45 R-N5 R-B6

44   R-K5   R-B6

-2.47 (1,568,177; 429; 9)

45 B-N4 R-B5

45   B-N4   R-B5

-1.55 (672,852; 184; 8)

46 R-K7 R-N5 ch 47 K-B2 N-R2
48 R×NP N-B3 49 B-B3

46   R-K7   R-B2

-1.20 (781,421; 217; 8)

47 R×KP N-Q2 48 R-K7 P-R5 49
K-N2 P-N5 50 NB-B3

47   R×KP   R-Q2

-1.23 (579,012; 157; 8)

48 K-N2 P-R5

48   R-K7   P-R5

-1.33 (754,845; 201; 9)

49 K-N2 P-N5 50 B-B5 K-B4 51
B-N4 P-N3 52 P-R4 K-N4

49   K-N2   P-N5

-1.34 (357,150; 99; 8)

50 K-R2 P-N3 51 P-R4 K-B4 52
B-B3 P-N6 ch 53 K-R3 R×P 54
K×P

50   K-R2?!

50 B-B5 would have preven-
ted ... P-N3.

50   ...   P-N3

-1.31 (468,777; 129; 8)

51 K-N2 R-Q1 52 B-K1 P-R6 53
K-N3 R×P 54 K×P

51   K-N2   R-Q1

-1.31 (536,589; 148; 8)

52 K-R2 K-N4 53 B-Q2 ch K-B4
54 B-B3 N-Q2 55 K-N2

Help! Black is beginning to untan-
gle his pieces.

52 P-R4   N-Q2

-1.45 (875,466; 246; 8)

53 B-B3 N-B4 54 R-N7 ch K-B4
55 R-B7 ch K-K3 56 R-B4

53   P-R5   N-B3

-1.63 (929,565; 244; 9)

54 P×P N-Q4 55 B-K1 N×R 56
P×N P-R6 ch 57 K-N3 R-K1

I was expecting 53 ...P×P 54
B×P R-QR1 and hoping that 55 B-
B3 might hold.

54 P×P

Material equality at last. Now I
thought I had a draw: if my opponent made one more mistake, then
maybe   ...

54   ...   N-Q4

-1.61 (900,747; 234; 9)

55 B-K1 N×R 56 P×N P-R6 ch
57 K-N3 R-K1 58 P-N7 K-B4

55   P-N7!

At this point in the proceedings the computer got sick and the doctors were called. Twenty-five minutes later, with the program still having plenty of time on its clock, it played

55   ...   N × R

-1.54 (491,772; 125; 8)

56 P×N R-K1 57 B-Q6 K-B2 58 P-N8=R R×R 59 B×R K×P

A brilliant decision. 55 ... N×B does nothing for Black, if only because of something like 56 R-K4 N-B3 57 R×P ch K-R4 58 R-QB4. Also 55 ... N-B5 ch 56 K-R1 looks good for White. CHESS 4.7 had probably found the only way for Black to draw!

56   P×N   R-KR1!

+0.03 (242,230; 58; 8)

57 B-B3 P-R6 ch 58 K-N3 R-K1 59 B-R5 K-B4

On 56 ... R-K1 57 B-R5 wins.

57   B-Q6   K-B3

-1.30 (294,755; 71; 9)

58 K-R2 K-K3 59 P-N8=Q R×Q

58   P-N8=Q   R×Q

-0.75 (397,940; 89; 11)

59 B×R K×P 60 B-B7 K-B2 61 B-Q8 P-R6 ch 62 K-N3 K-N6 63 K×P P-R7

59   B×R   K×P

-0.53 (383,817; 77; 12)

60 B-B7 K-B2 61 B-Q8 P-R6 ch 62 K-N3 K-N3 63 B-B7 K-N4

60   B-B4   K-B3

-0.57 (378,895; 76; 12)

61 B-Q6 K-B4 62 B-K7 P-R6 ch 63 K-N3 K-N3 64 B-Q6 K-N4

61   B-Q2   K-N3

-0.55 (549,063; 110; 12)

62 B-N4 K-N4 63 B-K7 ch K-R4 64 B-B6 P-R6 ch 65 K-N3

62   B-K1   K-N4

-0.53 (531,415; 106; 12)

63 K-R2 K-R4 64 B-N4 K-N3 65 B-K7 P-R6 ch

63   B-B2   K-R4

-0.47 (551,712; 111; 13)

64 K-R2 P-R6 65 B-N3 K-N3 66 B-B7 K-B4 67 K-N3 K-N4 68 B-N8 P-R7

64   B-K1

And David Slate offered me a **draw** on behalf of his program.

A remarkable game, and the first time a computer program has ever drawn with an international master under tournament conditions. Before the match David Slate had had some doubts as to whether his program was ready for me, but this game removed them.

The next day saw game two of the match, in which the program was faced with more difficult problems from an early stage.

GAME 2
White: CHESS 4.7
Black: Levy

Sicilian Defence

1 N-QB3(book)   P-QB4
2 P-K4(book)   N-QB3

3   P-B4(book)   P-QR3 +

To take the program out of the book. I have played this system as White several times and would not feel comfortable on the other side.

4   N-B3

David Cahlander and David Levy relaxing before a game.

+0.27 (534,448; 176; 7)

4 ... P-Q3 5 B-B4 N-R4 6 B-K2 B-Q2 7 0-0

4 ...   P-KN3
5 P-Q4

+0.40 (536,940; 177; 7)

5 ... P×P 6 N×P B-N2 7 B-K3 P-Q3 8 B-K2

5 ...   P×P
6 N×P

+0.42 (285,587; 92; 7)

6 ... B-N2 7 B-K3 N-R3 8 B-K2 0-0 9 0-0

6 ...   B-N2
7 B-K3

+0.36 (454,059; 146; 7)

7 ... P-K4 8 N×N NP×N 9 B-B4 P×P 10 B×BP

7 ...   P-Q3
8 N×N?

+0.31 (222,023; 69; 6)

8 ... P×N 9 B-K2 R-N1 10 B-Q4 P-K4

After making this strategic error against my Sicilian last year, the program was altered in an attempt to prevent it from exchanging in similar situations. Some of the factors causing this exchange were eradicated, but apparently not enough of them.

8 ...   P×N
9 B-K2

+0.10 (360,727; 115; 6)

9 ... R-N1 10 Q-B1 N-B3 11 B-Q4 P-B4

9 ...   R-N1
10 Q-B1

+0.04 (1,185,859; 395; 7)

10 ... B×N ch 11 P×B Q-R4 12 B-Q2 N-B3 13 P-B4

10 ...   Q-R4

11 B-Q2
+0.14 (239,111; 82; 6)
11 ... Q-N5 12 R-QN1 N-B3
13 P-K5 P×P 14 P×P
11 ... Q-N3
12 N-R4
+0.14 (267,191; 89; 6)
12 ... Q-N2 13 R-QN1 N-B3
14 B-B3 0-0
12 ... Q-R2
13 N-B3
+0.01 (271,911; 89; 6)
13 ... B-Q5 14 N-Q1 N-B3
15 P-B3 B-B4
13 ... B-Q5
14 N-Q1
-0.10 (732,542; 246; 7)
14 ... N-B3 15 P-B3 B-N3 16
Q-B2 B-N5 17 B×B N×B
14 ... N-B3
15 P-B3
-0.10 (524,256; 168; 7)
15 ... B-N3 16 Q-B2 B-Q2 17
P-B5 P×P 18 P×P
15 ... B-N3
16 Q-B2
-0.20 (1,444,961; 497; 7)
16 ... B-N5 17 B×B N×B 18
P-KR3 N-B7 19 N×N B×N ch 20
K-K2
16 ... N-N5
17 Q-R4
0.00 (262,998; 90; 6)
17 ... Q-N2 18 P-QR3 N-B3 19
P-K5 P×P 20 P×P
17 ... 0-0
18 B×N
+0.03 (1,082,139; 357; 7)
18 ... B×N 19 Q×BP B-N8
20 P-N4 QR-B1 21 Q-Q5
If 18 Q×BP N-B7 exchanging
knights and then bishops, and

White's exposed king must cost him
the game.
18 ... B×B
19 Q×BP
-0.23 (617,331; 202; 7)
19 ... B-N8 20 P-N4 B-R7 21
N-B2 B-Q2 22 Q-Q5
19 ... B×N
20 K×B
+0.37 (286,488; 85; 7)
20 ... B-K6 21 P-QN4 KR-B1
22 Q-Q5 R-N4 23 Q-N3
20 R×B B-K6 is equally horrible
for White.
20 ... B-K6
21 P-QN3
+0.33 (520,425; 157; 7)
21 ... B×B 22 K×B KR-B1
23 Q-R4 Q-B7 ch 24 K-Q3
21 ... B×B
22 K×B
-0.43 (949,692; 253; 8)
22 ... KR-B1 23 Q-R4 Q-B7 ch
24 K-Q3 Q×NP 25 QR-KB1 R-R1
22 ... QR-B1
23 Q-R4
-0.60 (849,366; 233; 8)
23 ... Q-B7 ch 24 K-Q3
Q×NP 25 P-B4 Q-B6 ch 26 K-Q4 P-
B4
23 ... Q-B7 ch
24 K-Q3
-1.16 (783,833; 227; 8)
24 ... Q×NP 25 Q-Q4 Q-B6
ch 26 K-B2 Q×P 27 QR-KB1 Q-N4
24 ... Q×NP
25 Q-Q4
-1.17 (360,866; 111; 7)
25 ... Q-B6 ch 26 K-B2 Q-K7
ch 27 K-N1 Q-N7 28 R-N1 Q×P
25 ... Q-B6 ch
26 K-B2

-1.27 (1,952;740; 571; 9)

26   ...   Q-K7 ch 27 K-B1 P-B4 28 P×P R×BP 29 Q-Q2 Q×Q ch 30 K×Q R×KBP

26   ...   Q-K7 ch
27   K-B1

-1.27 (422,483; 130; 7)

27   ...   P-B4 28 P×P R×P 29 Q-Q2 Q×Q ch 30 K×Q R×KBP

27   ...   P-K4
28   P×P

-0.46 (448,407; 128; 8)

28   ...   P×P 29 Q×P KR-K1 30 Q-QR5 R×P 31 P-B4 Q-N7

28   ...   P×P
29   Q×P

-1.02 (882,932; 263; 8)

29   ...   KR-Q1 30 Q-B4 R-Q6 31 Q-K5 KR-Q1 32 Q-QR5 Q×KP

29   ...   KR-K1
30   Q-N3

-0.57 (371,857; 104; 7)

30   ...   R×P 31 Q-R3 P-B4 32 P-B4 QR-K1 33 K-N1

30   ...   R×P
31   Q-R3

-2.21 (306,863; 89; 7)

31   ...   P-B4 32 K-N1 R-K6 33 Q-R4 R/K×P 34 R-K1

31   ...   R-Q1
32   Q-B1

-7.25 (518,359; 135; 8)

32   ...   Q-K6 ch 33 K-N1 R-Q7 34 R-N1 Q×P 35 R×P ch RP×R 36 Q×P R×KRP

32   ...   Q-Q7 ch
33   K-N1

-0.72 (142; 0; 2)

33   ...   P-B4

33   ...   R-K7
34   Q×R

-20.21 (477,123; 127; 8)

34   ...   Q×Q 35 R-K1 Q×R ch 36 K-N2 R-Q7 ch 37 K-R3 Q×R

34   ...   Q×Q
35   R-K1!

-21.71 (658,057; 146; 9)

35   ...   Q×R ch 36 K-N2 R-Q7 ch 37 K-R3 Q×R 38 K-N4 R×KRP 39 P-R3

Otherwise it is mate in four.

35   ...   Q×R ch
36   K-N2

-23.54 (624,008; 133; 9)

36   ...   R-Q7 ch 37 K-R3 Q-K4 38 P-N4 Q×P ch 39 K-R4 Q×R 40 P-R3 R×P

36   ...   R-Q7 ch
37   K-R3

-20.21 (80; 0; 2)

37   ...   Q×R

37   ...   Q×R

The remaining seventeen moves are of no interest. In all fairness to the program, I should say that it occasionally saw ways I could have forced mate which I myself did not see.

38   K-N4

mate in 7 (934,994; 239; 8)

38   ...   Q-K8 39 K-R4 Q-K1 40

K-R3 Q-K4 41 P-N4

38 ...   **P-R4 ch**

39 K-B4

mate in 6 (1,341,883; 344; 8)

39 ... Q-K8 40 P-N4 Q-K7 ch

39 ...   **Q-B8 ch**

40 K-B5

-21.66 (52; 0; 2)

40 ... R×KRP

40 ...   **Q-B4 ch**

41 K-B6

mate in 5 (91,249; 24; 6)

41 ... Q-K3 ch 42 K-N5 Q-K4 ch 43 K-R6 R-Q3 ch 44 K-R7 Q-K2 ch 45 K-R8 R-Q8 mate

41 ...   **Q-B1 ch**

42 K-N6

mate in 4 (5,205; 1; 4)

42 ... R-Q3 ch 43 K-N5 Q-B3 ch 44 K×P Q-B4 ch 45 K-R4 R-R3 mate

42 ...   **R-Q3 ch**

43 K-N5

mate in 3 (7,168; 2; 4)

43 ... Q-B3 ch 44 K×P Q-B4 ch 45 K-R4 R-R3 mate

43 ...   **Q-N2 ch**

44 K-R4

mate in 4 (743,709; 190; 8)

44 ... Q-B3 ch 45 K-R3 Q×P 46 P-R3 R-Q7 47 P-R4 Q-N5 mate

44 ...   **R-Q7**

45 P-N4

mate in 4 (1,033,390; 268; 8)

45 ... R×P ch 46 K-N3 Q-Q4 ch 47 P-B4 Q-Q7 48 P×P

45 ...   **R×P ch**

46 K-N3

mate in 3 (23; 0; 2)

46 ... R×P

46 ...   **Q-Q4 ch**

47 P-B4

mate in 2 (144; 0; 2)

47 ... Q-Q7 48 P×P Q×QRP

47 ...   **P-R5 ch**

48 K×R

mate in 3 (9,983; 2; 6)

48 ... Q-Q7 ch 49 K-R1 P-R6 50 P-R3 Q-N7 mate

48 ...   **Q×P ch**

49 K-N2

mate in 5 (502,918; 107; 9)

49 ... Q-Q6 50 K-B1 P-R6 51 P-N5 Q-K7 52 P-R3 P-R7 53 P-N6 P-R8=Q mate

49 ...   **Q-N6 ch**

50 K-B1

mate in 5 (418,175; 90; 9)

50 ... Q-R7 51 K-Q1 Q×P 52 K-B1 P-R6 53 K-Q1 P-R7 54 K-B1 P-R8=Q mate

50 ...   **P-R6**

51 K-Q2

mate in 4 (285,700; 65; 8)

51 ... P-R7 52 K-K2 P-R8=Q 53 P-R3 Q-KN8 54 K-Q2 Q/8-Q8 mate

51 ...   **P-R7**

52 K-K2

mate in 3 (62,883; 15; 6)

52 ... P-R8=Q 53 P-R3 Q-KN8 54 K-Q2 Q/8-Q8 mate

52 ...   **P-R8=Q**

53 K-B2

mate in 2 (31,274; 8; 4)

53 ... Q/8-Q8 54 P-R4

53 ...   **Q/8-R7 ch**

54 K-K1

mate in 1 (266; 0; 2)

54 ... Q/6-N8 mate

54 ...   **Q/6-N8 mate**

After the second game there was a five-day break before hostilities resumed. In game three my do-nothing-but-do-it-well strategy scored another convincing victory.

GAME 3
White: Levy
Black: CHESS 4.7

English Opening

1	P-QB4	N-KB3
		(book)
2	P-QR3	

Out of the book again.

2   ...   N-B3
-0.22 (331,999; 112; 7)

3 N-KB3 P-Q4 4 P×P N×P 5 P-K4 N-B5

3   N-QB3   P-Q4
-0.24 (380,122; 126; 7)

4 P×P N×P 5 N-B3 B-B4 6 P-Q4 P-K3

4   P×P   N×P
-0.22 (184,293; 58; 7)

5 P-Q4 P-K4 6 P×P N×N 7 Q×Q ch K×Q 8 P×N N×P

5   P-Q3
To encourage

5   ...   N×N
-0.35 (330,662; 96; 7)

6 P×N P-K4 7 N-B3 B-K2 8 R-QN1 0-0

... as in game two.

6   P×N   P-K4
-0.26 (217,302; 71; 7)

7 N-B3 B-K2 8 P-K4 B-KN5 9 B-K3 0-0

7   P-N3   B-K2
-0.30 (305,903; 102; 6)

8 B-N2 B-KN5 9 R-N1 Q-B1 10 B×N ch P×B

8   B-N2   Q-Q3
-0.20 (405,822; 137; 6)

9 Q-N3 0-0 10 B-K3 K-R1 11 B-K4

9   N-B3   B-K3
-0.21 (630,434; 215; 6)

10 N-N5 0-0 11 0-0

10   0-0   0-0
-0.16 (432,068; 147; 6)

11 B-Q2 P-B4 12 Q-N1 QR-N1 13 N-N5 B×N 14 B×B

11   Q-R4
Intending to put pressure on the QNP with KR-N1

11   ...   Q-B4
-0.23 (418-702; 145; 6)

12 B-Q2 P-QN4 13 Q-B2 P-B3 14 B-K3

12   B-Q2   P-QN4?
-0.15 (808, 838; 275; 6)

13 Q-B2 P-B3 14 P-K4 N-Q4 15 N×N P×N

A typical program failing; it weakens its pawn structure without sufficient provocation.

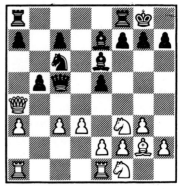

13   Q-B2   P-B3
-0.04 (753,664; 249; 7)

14 B-K3 Q-Q3 15 P-QR4 P-N5 16 N-Q2 P-QR4 17 P×P N×P
14 KR-N1   QR-Q1
-0.24 (572,717; 198; 6)
15 R-KB1 P-QR4 16 K-R1 Q-N3 17 P-B4
15 Q-N2
Not 15 B-K3 N-Q5! 16 Q-N2 Q×BP!
15 ...   R-N1
-0.23 (252,760; 79; 6)
16 B-K3 Q-Q3 17 N-Q2 P-QR3 18 N-K4
16 B-K3   Q-Q3
-0.24 (522,533; 175; 7)
17 Q-B2 P-QR4 18 R-KB1 P-B4 19 N-N5 P-B5 20 N×B Q×N
17 N-Q2
Intending N-N3 or N-K4, followed by N-B5 or B-B5.
17 ...   B-Q4
-0.23 (204,311; 62; 6)
18 N-K4 Q-Q1 19 N-B5 P-B4 20 N-K6 B×N 21 B×N
18 B×B ch   Q×B
-0.14 (568,218; 175; 8)
19 Q-B2 P-QR3 20 P-QR4 P-B4 21 P-QB4 P×BP 22 Q×P
19 Q-N3
The program can analyse far more deeply in the ending than in the middlegame because there are fewer pieces on the board and also fewer possible moves. For this reason I usually try to avoid the endgame until the program has compromised its position - which it has done here. I felt that Black's poor pawn structure would soon prove fatal.
19 ...   Q×Q
-0.26 (246,373; 73; 8)
20 N×Q P-B4 21 R-KB1 P-QR4

22 P-B3 P-R4 23 N-Q2
20 N×Q   P-B4
-0.21 (254,511; 76; 7)
21 P-QR4 P-QR5 22 P×P R×P 23 N-Q2 R×R ch 24 R×R
21 B-B5   B-Q3!
-0.21 (336,741; 99; 7)
22 K-R1 P-QR4 23 B×B P×B 24 N-Q2 P-Q4
The exchange on B4 would permit White's knight to enter the game with great effect.
22 R-N2   K-R1
-0.26 (760,764; 232; 7)
23 QR-N1 P-QR3 24 P-K4 P×P 25 P×B B×B 26 N×B
When it does not know what else to do the program puts its king "into safety". CHESS 4.7 is aware that the king should be nearer the corner in the middlegame and centralised in the endgames. I suppose the threshold between middle- and endgame is not sufficiently defined - the program thinks it is still in the middlegame.
23 QR-N1   P-QR3
-0.27 (424,892; 126; 7)
24 P-B3 P-B5 25 K-R1 N-K2 26 P-N4 B×B 27 N×B
24 B×B   P×B
-0.33 (228,547; 67; 7)
25 N-Q2 P-B5 26 P-B4 N-Q5 27 P-K4 P×NP 28 RP×P
25 N-Q2   P-B5
-0.26 (332,840; 100; 7)
26 P-K4 P×P e.p. 27 P×P P-Q4 28 R-KB1 N-K2 29 R×R ch R×R
26 K-N2   P×P
-0.27 (706,961; 211; 7)
27 RP×P QR-Q1 28 P-QB4 P×P 29 N×P P-Q4 30 R-N6 R-B1

27   RP × P   QR-Q1
-0.13 (697,027; 202; 7)
28 P-QB4 P × P 29 N × P P-Q4 30
R-N6 R-B1

28   P-R4!   N-R2!
-0.04 (302,424; 83; 7)
29 R-QR1 P × P 30 R × P N-N4 31
N-K4 R-R1

Perceiving that 28   ...   P × P 29
R-N6 would be extremely unpleasant for Black.

29   N-K4   P × P
-0.02 (701,727; 188; 8)
30 R-N6 P-Q4 31 N-B5 N-N4 32
N × P/4 R-R1 33 R-N7

30   R-N6   P-Q4
+0.17 (583,538; 152; 8)
31 N-B5 N-N4 32 N × P/4 R-R1 33
P-QB4 N-R6 34 R/1-N3

31   N-B5   N-N4
+0.23 (942,370; 258; 8)
32 N × P/4 R-QR1 33 R-K6 KR-
K1 34 R × R ch R × R 35 P-QB4

32   N × P/4   R-QR1
+0.16 (496,625; 144; 7)
33 R-N2 P-K5 34 P × P P × P 35 P-
QB4 N-Q4

33   P-QB4
Remember what I said about
passed pawns!

33   ...   P × P
+0.42 (635,379; 163; 8)
34 P × P N-R6 35 R-QB1 QR-B1
36 P-B5 P-QR4 37 R-B3

34   P × P   N-Q5
+0.53 (970,480; 264; 8)
35 P-K3 N-B6 36 P-B5 N-Q7 37
R-Q1 N-B5 38 R-N7

35   P-K3   N-B6
+0.60 (2,637,333; 730; 9)
36 P-B5 N-N4 37 R-N7 N-K5 38
P-B4 P × P 39 KP × P QR-Q1

36   P-B5   N-N4
+0.60 (476,059; 135; 7)
37 R-N7 N-K5 38 P-B4 P × P 39
KP × P QR-Q1

Or 36   ...   N-Q7 37 R-N4 and
the Black knight has nothing to do.

37   P-B6   N-K5
+0.56 (391,981; 112; ;7)
38 P-B4 P × P 39 NP × P N-Q7 40
R-QR1 N-B5

38   P-B7   R × P ch
-0.02 (1,379,960; 397; 8)
39 K-N1 KR-KB-1 40 R-N8 N × P
41 R/1-N4

With this move the program
warned "Be careful!" (but I was not
told of this until after the game). In
fact, Black has no defence to the
threat of 39 R-N8 ch in conjunction
with N-N6.

39   K-N1   KR-B1
-0.63 (879,932; 252; 7)
40 R-QB6 QR-B1 41 N-N6 N-Q7
42 R/1-QB1 N-B6ch 43 K-N2

40   R-N8   P-KR4
+9.46 (460,002; 114; 8)
41 R × R R × R 42 R-N8 ch K-R2
43 P-B8 = Q R × R 44 Q × R N × P
45 Q × P

41   R × R   R × R
+11.61 (787,096; 176; 10)
42 R-N8 ch K-R2 43 R × R N-Q3
44 R-Q8 N-B1 45 R × N K-N3 46 N-
B5

42   R-N8 ch   K-R2
+15.55 (794,632; 178; 10)
43 R × R N-Q3 44 R-Q8 N-K5 45
P-B8 = Q N × P 46 K-N2 P-R5 47 R-
R8 ch K-N3 48 R × P

David Slate resigned for his
program.

I now had a lead of $2\frac{1}{2}$-$\frac{1}{2}$ and needed only one draw in the last three games to win my bet. I had demonstrated to everyone's satisfaction that my do-nothing strategy worked to perfection, so I considered it worthwhile to experiment in game four by attempting to beat the program at its own game, playing sharp, tactical chess and endeavoring to outanalyze CHESS 4.7. This was the result.

GAME 4
White: CHESS 4.7
Black: Levy

Latvian Gambit

1	P-K4(book)	P-K4
2	N-KB3(book)	P-KB4
3	P×P	

+0.76 (455,388: 153; 7)

3 ... P-K5 4 N-K5 K-KB3 5 B-N5 Q-K2 6 N-B4

3	...	P-K5
4	N-K5	

+1.06 (647,160; 215; 7)

4 ... Q-N4 5 Q-N4 Q×Q 6 N×Q N-KB3 7 N×N ch P×N

4	...	N-KB3
5	N-N4	

+0.53 (211,585; 69; 6)

5 ... N-B3 6 N-QB3 N×N 7 Q×N P-Q4

5	...	P-Q4
6	N×N ch	

+0.76 (268,819; 88; 7)

6 ...Q×N 7 Q-R5 ch K-Q1 8 N-B3 P-Q5 9 N-N5

6	...	Q×N
7	Q-R5 ch	

+0.55 (189,803; 64; 7)

7 ... K-Q1 8 N-B3 P-B3 9 P-KN4 P-KN3 10 P×P P×P 11 N×P P×N 12 Q×P ch B-Q3 13 Q×KP R×P 14 R×R B×R

The program is a pawn up and is thus quite willing to trade queens.

7	...	Q-B2

8	Q×Q ch	K×Q
9	N-B3	P-B3
10	P-Q3	

+0.62 (300,808; 92; 7)

10 ... B×P 11 P×P B×P 12 N×B P×N 13 B-B4

10	...	P×P
11	B×P	

+1.34 (341,668; 106; 7)

11 ... N-Q2 12 B-KB4 N-B4 13 P-KN4 K-N1 14 0-0 N×B 15 P×N

11	...	N-Q2
12	B-KB4	

+1.34 (642,724; 198; 7)

12 ... K-N1 13 0-0 N-B4 14 P-KN4 N×B 15 P×N

12	...	N-B4
13	P-KN4	

+0.32 (287,237; 86; 7)

13 ...P-KR4 14 B-K2 P×P 15 P-N4 N-R3 16 B×N P×B

13	...	N×B ch
14	P×N	

+0.13 (318,041; 88; 8)

14 ...P-KR4 15 P-B3 P×P 16 P×P R-R5 17 R-KB1 R×NP

14	...	B-B4

Preventing 0-0-0 and therefore encouraging 0-0; the program likes to castle when its pieces have been developed.

15	0-0	

+1.20 (592,278; 182; 7)

15 ... P-QN3 16 N-R4 B-K2 17 QR-Q1 B-R3 18 KR-K1

15   ...   **P-KR4**
16   **N-R4**
+0.26 (422,519; 125; 7)
16   ...B-Q5 17 B-K3 B×B 18
P×B P×P 19 N-B5
16   ...   **B-Q5**
17   **B-K3**
+0.16 (750,709; 200; 8)
17   ...   B×B 18 P×B P×P 19
P-K4 R-R6 20 N-B5 P-QN3
17   ...   **B-K4**
18   **P-Q4**
+1.06 (497,290; 153; 7)
18   ...   B-Q3 19 P-KR3 P-QN3
20 KR-B1 B-Q2 21 B-N5 P×P 22
P×P
18   ...   **B-Q3**
19   **P-KR3**
+0.77 (337,183; 106; 7)
19   ...   R-K1 20 KR-K1 K-N1 21
B-Q2 B-Q7 22 N-B5 B×N 23 P×B
19   ...   **P-QN3**
20   **KR-K1**
+1.02 (770,702; 236; 7)
20   ...   P×P 21 P×P B-R3 22
B-N5 K-N1 23 QR-B1
20   ...   **B-Q2**
21   **N-B3**
+0.72 (169,446; 51; 6)
21   ...   P×P 22 P×P R-R5 23
P-B3 R-R7
21   ...   **P×P**
22   **P×P**
+0.60 (368,992; 108; 7)
22   ...   R-R5 23 P-B3 R-R7 24
B-B2 QR-R1 25 K-B1
22   ...   **R-R5**
23   **P-B3**
+0.35 (234,136; 67; 7)
23   ...   QR-R1 24 K-B1 R-R6 25
K-K2 R-R7 26 B-B2
23   ...   **QR-R1**

24   **K-B1!**
+0.32 (412,942; 120; 7)
24   ...   R-R6 25 K-K2 R-R7
ch26 B-B2 K-N1 27 K-B1

24   ...   **B-N6?**
The immediate 24   ...   B-QB1 is
better, and if 25 K-K2 (even worse
for White is 25 N-K2 B-R3)
25   ...   R-R7 ch 26 K-Q1 (not 26
B-B2?? B-N6 27 R-KB1 R-K1 ch
winning a piece) 26   ...   R×P with
an overwhelming position.
25   **R-K2**
+0.54 (292,595; 84; 7)
25   ...   R-R8 ch 26 B-N1 B-Q3
27 QR-K1 K-N1 28 P-N3
25   ...   **B-QB1**
26   **K-N2**
+0.75 (356,720; 103; 7)
26   ...R-R6 27 B-N1 B-R3 28 R-
K6 B-N2 29 N-K2
26   ...   **B-Q3**
27   **B-N1**
+0.54 (226,239; 67; 7)
27   ...   B-Q2 28 QR-K1 K-N1
29 K-B1 R-R8 30 P-N3
27   ...   **R-R6**
28   **QR-K1**
+0.60 (744,584; 223; 7)

28 ... B-Q2 29 P-R3 K-N1 30 P-N4 R-R8 31 K-B1

28 ... R-N6 ch

29 K-B2

+0.45 (252,687; 74; 7)

29 ... R/N-R6 30 R-Q1 B-B5 31 P-N4 B-QR3 32 R/Q-K1

29 ... R/R-R6

30 R-K3

+1.01 (448,775; 135; 7)

30 ... B-R3 31 N-K2 B×N 32 R/1×B P-B4 33 P×P B×P

30 ... B-R3

If 30 ... B-B5 31 R-K7 ch K-B3 32 R/1-K3! with N-K2 to follow. Had I noticed these defensive resources earlier I would have played 24 ... B-QB1.

31 N-K2

+0.77 (238,329; 68; 7)

31 ... B×N 32 R/1×B P-B4 33 R-R3 P×P 34 R×P ch K-N1

31 ... B×N

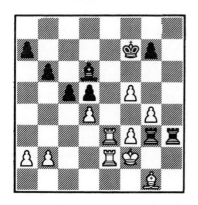

32 R/1×B

+0.66 (228,450; 65; 7)

32 ... P-B4 33 R-R3 P-R4 34 R-K6 B-B5 35 R×NP P×P

32 ... P-B4

33 P-B4!

+0.14 (541,278; 158; 8)

33 ... R×R 34 R×R R×R 35 K×R P×P ch 36 K-Q3 B×P 37 B×P

I have overlooked this move.

33 ... R×R

34 R×R

+0.24 (1,233,406; 334; 10)

34 ... R×R 35 K×R P×P ch 36 K-Q3 K-N1 37 B×P B×P 38 P-N3 K-B2

34 ... R-R5

34 ... R×R 35 K×R P×P ch 36 K-Q3! gives White a won bishop ending.

35 K-N3

+1.06 (842,547; 233; 9)

35 ... R-R8 36 B-B2 P×P 37 R-Q3 R-QB8 38 B×P R-B7 39 K-B3

35 ... R-R8

36 B-B2

+1.17 (369,782; 105; 8)

36 ... P×P 37 R-Q3 R-KB8 38 R×P B-B4 39 R-Q2 B×B ch 40 R×B R×R 41 K×R

36 ... R-Q8!

37 R-R3

+1.43 (847,921; 237; 9)

37 ... P×P 38 R×P ch K-B1 39 K-B3 R-Q7 40 R-Q7 B-B4 41 R×P R×P 42 B×P B×B 43 R×B R×P

37 ... P×P

38 R×P ch

+2.34 (503,780;' 143; 9)

38 ... B-K2 39 K-B3 R-Q7 40 R-N7 P-Q6 41 B-R4 R-K7 42 B×B R×B 43 R×P ch

38 ... K-B1??

38 ... K-K1 39 R×P P-Q6 40

K-K3 R-QN8 would probably have been sufficient to win.

39   R-Q7

+2.53 (699,230; 188; 9)

39   ...   R-Q6 ch 40 K-N2 R-B4 41 R×P R-Q7 42 P-N4 B-K2 43 R×P R-N7

39   ...   R-Q6 ch??

An idea that fails because of White's 48th move. Correct is 39 ... B-B4 40 R×P P-Q6 41 B×B ch P×B when CHESS 4.7 would almost certainly not have been able to win; it may even have lost because of the passed Q-pawn.

40   K-N2

+1.61 (1,285,544; 337; 10)

40   ...   B×P 41 R×P B-K6 42 B×B R×B 43 R×P R-K7 ch 44 K-B3 R×P

40   ...   B-B4

41   R×P

+2.66 (656,375; 172; 9)

41   ...   R-Q7 42 P-N4 B-K2 43 R×P P×P 44 K-B3 P-QN4 45 R-K4

41   ...   R-Q7

42   P-N4

+2.75 (474,441; 126; 9)

42   ...   B-K7 43 K-B3 R×P 44 B×P B×P 45 B×P K-K2 46 R-Q4

42   ...   B×P

43   R-Q8 ch

+2.74 (800,572; 212; 9)

43   ...   K-B2 44 R×P R-N7 45 R-Q7 ch B-K2 46 R-R7 R-B7 47 K-B3

43   ...   K-B2

44   R-Q7 ch

+1.54 (1,774,804; 498; 9)

44   ...   B-K2 45 K-B3 K-K1 46 R×P R×P 47 R-Q5 R-R6 ch 48 K-K4

44   ...   K-B1

45   R×QP

+3.03 (290, 158; 77; 8)

45   ...   R-N7 46 K-B3 B-K2 47 R-R4 B-B4 48 R-R8 ch K-B2

45   ...   R-N7

46   K-B3

+2.67 (629,351; 165; 9)

46   ...   B-B4 47 R-Q8 ch K-B2 48 B×B P×B 49 R-Q7 ch K-B3 P-R4

46   ...   B-B4

47   R-Q8 ch

+2.66 (957,241; 234; 10)

47   ...   K-B2 48 B×B P×B 49 R-Q7 ch K-B3 50 P-R4 R-QR7 51 R-R7 P-B5

47   ...   K-K2??

The final blunder. I had still not noticed White's next move and assumed that the program was going to play 48 B×B ch, when either 48 ... P×B or 48 ... K×R 49 B-Q4 R×P 50 B×KNP would produce the unbalanced type of endgame at which the program fares less well due to its inferior understanding of passed pawns.

After 47 ... K-B2 I don't think the program could have won.

48   B-R4 ch!

+3.22 (359,796; 90; 9)

48   ...   K-B2 49 P-N5 P-N3 50 P×P ch K×P 51 R-QR8 K-B4 52 R-R7

The end.

48   ...   K-B2

49   P-N5

+4.13 (583,453; 156; 9)

49   ...   P-N3 50 R-Q7 ch K-B1 51 P×P R×P 52 P-B5 P-N4 53 K-B4

49 ...   P-N3
50   R-Q7 ch
+ 4.17 (1,184,309; 294; 10)
50   ...   K-N1 51 P×P R×P 52
P-B5 P-N4 53 P-B6 P-N5 54 R-Q8
ch B-B1
50   ...   K-B1
51   P×P
+ 4.31(520,678; 136; 9)
51   ...   R×P 52 P-B5 R-R6 ch
53 K-N4 R-R5 ch 54 K-R5 P-N4 55
B-N3
51   ...   R×P
52   P-B5
+ 4.40 (1,055,542; 283; 9)
52   ...   R-R6 ch 53 K-N4 R-R5
ch 54 K-R5 P-N4 55 P-B6 R-K5 56
B-N3
52   ...   R-R6 ch
53   K-N4
+ 4.50 (1,751,564; 473; 10)

53   ...   R-R5 ch 54 K-R5 R-Q5
55 R-QN7 R-Q1 56 P-B6 K-N1 57
R-N7 ch K-B1
53   ...   R-R5 ch
54   K-R5
+ 4.67 (938,513; 247; 10)
54   ...   R-Q5 55 R-KR7 R-KB5
56 P-B6 K-N1 57 P-B7 ch K-B1 58
R-R8 ch K-K2 59 R-K8 ch K-Q2
54   ...   R-Q5
55   R-B7
+ 7.43 (2,260,258; 579; 10)
55   ...   R×B ch 56 K×R K-N1
57 P-B6 B-B7 ch 58 K-N4
55   ...   B-K2
56   P-B6
+ 8.43 (564,536; 130; 9)
56   ...   B-Q1 57 P-N7 ch K-N1
58 K-N6 B×P 59 P×B R-N5 ch 60
B-N5
56   ...   **Black resigns.**

So the experiment failed, but computer persons all over the world will finally have something to rejoice about.

For the fifth game I returned to my no-nonsense approach.

GAME 5
White: Levy
Black: CHESS 4.7

English Opening
1   P-QB4   N-KB3(book)
2   P-QR3   P-B3(book)

Slate added this move to the program's openings library after the third game.

3   P-Q3   P-Q4(book)
4   Q-B2

No, I am not mad: there is a perfectly valid reason for these moves. In a blitz game between CHESS 4.6 and GM Michael Stean

in London 1977, the program opened 1 P-K4 P-QN3 2 P-Q4 B-N2 3 N-QB3 P-QB4 4 P×P. If the program likes to exchange centre pawns for wing pawns, who am I to stop it?

4   ...   P×P
-0.23 (159,200; 53; 6)
5 P×P P-K3 6 P-K4 B-QB4 7 Q-Q3 Q×Q 8 B×Q

5   Q×P   P-K4
-0.23 (262,590; 88; 6)
6 N-KB3 B-K3 7 Q-B3 P-K5 8 N-K5

So now I have a Sicilian pawn structure!

6   N-KB3   B-Q3

-0.33 (1,378,458; 463; 7)

7 QN-Q2 0-0 8 Q-KR4 P-QN4 9 N-K4 N×N 10 Q×N

7   P-KN3   B-K3

-0.35 (481,922; 166; 6)

8 Q-KR4 QN-Q2 9 B-R3 B×B 10 Q×B

8   Q-B2   QN-Q2

-0.36 (397,130; 133; 6)

9 B-N2 Q-N3 10 B-K3 B-N6 11 Q-B3

9   B-N2   0-0

-0.34 (486,236; 164; 6)

10 0-0 Q-N3

10   0-0   Q-N3

-0.23 (347,711; 116; 6)

11 B-K3 B-N6 12 Q-B3 N-Q4 13 B×Q N×Q 14 N×N P×B

11   QN-Q2   Q-B4

-0.20 (240,297; 72; 6)

12 N-B4 B×N 13 P×B P-QN4 14 P-N3

12   Q-N1

I wanted to keep the queens on the board as long as I could to force the program to examine as many moves as possible at each level; its search would therefore be shallower than otherwise.

12   ...   P-KR3

-0.34 (319, 129; 100; 6)

13 N-K4 N×N 14 P×N P-B3 15 B-K3

13   P-QN4   Q-N4

-0.27 (248,491; 80; 6)

14 Q-B2 N-N5 15 B-N2 B-K2 16 P-R3

14   Q-B2   N-N3

-0.21 (827,004; 297; 6)

15 B-N2 P-QR4 16 QR-N1 N-N5 17 N-K4

15   B-N2   P-QR4

-0.11 (906,758; 327; 6)

16 P-Q4 P-K5 17 N×P N×N 18 Q×N P×P

16   P-QR4   Q-R3

-0.25 (242,170; 75; 6)

17 P×P Q×RP 18 B-B3 Q-B4 19 P-R5

17   P×P   Q×RP

-0.02 (2,037,120; 663; 7)

18 N-N3 B×N 19 Q×B P-K5 20 N-R4 P×P 21 Q×QP

The game is becoming sharper than I had intended, but with Black's queen offside I was very happy with the situation.

18   B-B3   Q-B4

-0.16 (322,247; 103; 6)

19 N-N3 B×N 20 Q×B N×P 21 B×P B×B 22 R×N R×R 23 Q×R

19   KR-B1   QN-Q2

-0.21 (754,910; 258; 6)

20 P-K3 KR-Q1 21 Q-Q1 Q-R2 22 N-B4

The threat was simply 20 B×P.

20   P-R5   Q-R2

-0.40 (371, 312; 137; 5)

21 R-B1 Q-R3 22 K-R1 N-Q4

21 Q-N2   N-N5

-0.27 (215,498; 81; 5)

22 P-Q4 B-Q4 23 P-R3 B × N 24 N × B

22 N-K4   B-B2

-0.36 (255,626; 99; 5)

23 B-N4 P-KB4 24 N-B5 KR-K1

22 ... P-KB4 23 N × B Q × P ch 24 K-R1 leaves Black with insufficient compensation for the piece.

23 P-R3   P-KB4

-0.24 (361,794; 129; 6)

24 P × N P × N 25 P × P B × NP 26 B-N4

24 P × N   P × N

-0.22 (197, 085; 69; 6)

25 P × P B × NP 26 R-Q1 P-B4 27 Q-N3 ch K-R2

25 P × P   B × NP

-0.23 (186,831; 71; 5)

26 R-Q1 B-K3 27 P-K3 B-N5

26 B-K1

Unnecessary overprotection. The immediate 26 KR-N1 was stronger, but Black cannot easily prevent White's plan anyway.

26 ...   N-B4

27 KR-N1

At this point the computer became indisposed and required twenty-five minutes' consultation with its medical team. When it had recovered, only twenty minutes remained for the thirteen moves to the time control, but CHESS 4.7 managed to find the best defensive moves that I could see in the position.

27 ...   QR-K1

-0.40 (115,603; 40; 5)

28 Q-B2 B × N 29 P × B R-Q1

28 B-Q2

The point. White will put pressure on the Black knight defending QN2.

28 ...   R-B2

-0.24 (246,864; 92; 5)

29 Q-B2 N-Q2 30 Q-N2 B × N 31 P × B

If 28 ... N × P 29 B-K3 Q-R3 (29 ... N-B4 30 R-QB1 B-Q3 31 Q-B2) 30 Q × NP Q × KP 31 Q × B R-B2 32 Q × P forking rook and knight.

29 B-K3   B-Q3

-0.15 (231,595; 84; 5)

30 Q-B2 B × N 31 P × B QR-KB1

30 Q-B2   B × N

+0.12 (454,716; 152; 6)

31 P × B R-R1 32 R-QB1 P-QN3 33 P × P Q × R 34 R × Q R × R ch 35 B-KB1

31 B × B   R-R1

+1.34 (167,734; 57; 5)

32 R-Q1 B-K2 33 QR-B1 P-QN3 34 P × P

32 R-QB1   P-QN3

+1.02 (115,827; 39; 5)

33 Q-N2 P × P 34 Q-B3 R × B 35 P × R

33 K-N2

If 33 P × P Q × R 34 R × Q B × R ch 35 K-N2 R-R4, it is not immediately clear that White can win.

33 ...   Q-N2

+1.02 (113,042; 37; 5)

34 Q-B4 K-B1 35 B × N P × B

34 P × P   R × R

+1.54 (124,580; 37; 6)

35 R × R N-K3 36 R-R7 Q-B1 37 R × R K × R

35 R × R   N-K3

+1.61 (142,725; 49; 6)

36 R-R7 Q-B1 37 B-R5 R-B1 38 Q-Q1

36 R-R7   Q-B1

+3.10 (458,007;131; 7)

37 Q-B4 R-B3 38 P-N7 Q-K1 39 R-R6

37   Q-R2   R-B3

+2.15 (177,738; 51; 6)

38 R-R8 B-N1 39 B-N4 K-B2 40 B-QB5

38   R-R8   B-N1

+5.01 (296,439; 86; 7)

39 B-N4 K-B2 40 Q-R7 ch B×Q 41 R×Q B×P 42 B×B

39   B-N4   K-B2

+5.01 (722,578; 206; 7)

40 Q-R7 ch B×Q 41 R×Q B×P 42 B×B R-N3

40   Q-R7 ch   B×Q

+5.24 (1,010,509; 258; 10)

41 R×Q B×P 42 B×B K-K2 43 R-QR8 R-B2 44 B-KR5 R-B1 45 R-R7 ch K-Q3

41   R×Q   B×P

+5.26 (602,264; 157; 9)

42 B×B K-K2 43 B-KR5 K-Q3 44 B-N4 K-Q2 45 R-QR8 R-N3

42   B×N ch   R×B

+5.24 (903,909; 230; 10)

43 B×B K-B3 44 R-B7 K-N3 45 B-B5 K-R2 46 R-R7 K-N3 47 K-B3

43 B×B

Once again the computer failed and David Slate decided to resign the game and the match.

Thus ended an era in the annals of computer chess. I had proved that my 1968 assessment had been correct, but on the other hand my opponent in this match was very, very much stronger than I had believed possible when I started the bet. When sending me his cheque for £250 Professor John McCarthy expressed a sentiment with which I concurred - he said that had I lost to a brute force program he would not have felt that the science of Artificial Intelligence was responsible for my defeat. McCarthy, Michie and Papert all paid promptly and with good sportsmanship, just as I would have done had I lost the bet. Only Edward Kozdrowicki did not. At the time of going to press (Autumn 1979) he has had more than a year to pay but has refused all attempts to persuade him to do so.

In order to stimulate further work in computer chess I have decided to offer a prize of $1,000 US to the first programming team who writes a program that beats me in a four or six game match. The magazine **Omni** has generously added $4,000 to my own offer so there is now a $5,000 prize, with no time limit, waiting for someone. In addition to this offer I am prepared to wager up to $10,000 U.S. that no-one collects the prize before January 1st 1984. Up to now I have not had any takers but one person has told me that he is considering it - Claude Shannon, the father of computer chess.

Courtesy of United States Chess Federation, Chess Life & Review, *Vol. XXXII, No. 6.*

2 The State of the Art

In this chapter I shall illustrate the progress that has been made in computer chess during recent years by giving some of the better games played by the Northwestern University program and pinpointing some of the program's better results. I shall also comment on some specific areas where, in my opinion, little or no progress has been made.

The chapter on computer chess tournaments in my earlier book *Chess and Computers* shows the state of the art five yeas ago (summer 1974). At that time CHESS 4.0 had played some interesting games but none of which a strong club player could be proud. Within a year that statement was no longer true. At the 1975 ACM tournament in Minneapolis, CHESS 4.4, the latest version of the program, won a game against CHAOS which, in my opinion, remains to this day the best game ever played between two computer programs. In my book of that event I gave this game with copious notes which I intend to repeat here (with apologies to anyone who already owns the book of the 1975 event).

White: CHAOS
Black: CHESS 4.4

Modern Benoni

David Slate and Larry Atkin kindly supplied me with a copy of CHESS 4.4's printout and so I am able to give a lot of information that is not normally included in the annotation of a computer game. This information includes:

1) The CPU time (in seconds) taken to compute each move;
2) The number of positions examined in computing the move;
3) The program's current assessment of the position—a positive score indicates that the program considers the position to be better for White, and 64 evaluation points are roughly equivalent to one pawn;
4) The sequence of moves predicted by CHESS 4.4 (i.e. the continu-

ation that the program considers to represent best play for both sides).

This information is given *in italics* in order to distinguish it from my own comments.

1	P-Q4	N-KB3
1	P-QB4	P-B4
3	P-Q5	P-K3
4	N-QB3	P×P
5	P×P	P-Q3
6	P-K4	P-KN3
7	B-K2	

This move took CHESS 4.4 out of its openings book, since the move expected by CHESS 4.4 was 7 N-B3 when 7...B-N2 is met by 8 B-K2. After CHESS 4.4's next move and CHAOS' reply, the game is back in book so far as CHESS 4.4 is concerned. From CHAOS' point of view the opening never leaves book until move fifteen.

| 7 | ... | **B-N2** |

CPU time: 172 seconds
positions: 213,130
assessment: 30
predicting: 8 B-KB4 0-0 9 N-B3 B-N5 10 0-0

| 8 | **N-B3** | **0-0** |
| 9 | **0-0** | **R-K1** |

While CHESS 4.4 is still in book it naturally takes no time to compute its move and it does not examine the game tree, assess the current position or predict the forthcoming continuation.

10	**N-Q2**	**N-R3**
11	**P-B3**	**N-B2**
12	**P-QR4**	**P-N3**
13	**N-B4**	**B-QR3**
14	**B-N5**	**P-R3**
15	**B-R4**	

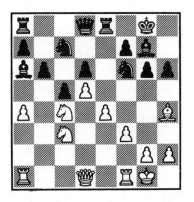

From here on, both programs are thinking for themselves. It would perhaps be as well to make some general comments concerning this variation of the Benoni. White's strategy revolves around his attempt to keep a firm grip on the centre and to prepare the advance P-K5. If this advance can be effected without conceding anything, White normally has a clear advantage. Black therefore keeps an eye on his K4 square to prevent White's breakthrough, and at the same time Black tries for counterplay on the Q-side, based on the advance ...P-QN4. If Black can play this advance with impunity before White makes any progress in the centre (or on the K-side), then it is Black who will get the advantage.

These are the considerations that would affect the choice of moves of a human player, but while both programs "know" this variation up to move fifteen, neither of them "understands" it. In my opinion it is at least as important to teach programs the ideas behind the openings as it is to teach them the openings themselves. One simple way in which this could be done is to store the general ideas behind a variation, as well as specific thematic moves, with each of the opening variations in the program's library. This would enable programs to give more than a cursory glance at the thematic moves and it would help them to find moves that conformed to the general requirements of the position. In this variation, for example, Black should always be considering the feasibility of playing ...P-QN4 and a general Q-side advance.

| 15 | ... | **P-KN4** |

CPU time: 115 seconds
positions: 129,779
assessment: 18
predicting: 16 B-B2 N-R4 17 Q-Q2 N-B5

Ken Thompson (center) follows his program's progress in a game against the Northern University program. David Cahlander and David Slate have their backs to the camera.

The usual move here is 15...Q-Q2.

16 B-B2

Weaker is 16 B-N3, putting pressure on Black's QP, but then Black can continue with either 16...B×N 17 B×B P-R3, followed by ...Q-Q2 and an early ...P-QN4; or 16...N-R4 and now:

(i) 17 N×QP B×N (or 17...B×B 18 N×B N×B 19 N×R N×Nch 20 Q×N Q×R and Black has the advantage of bishop and knight for rook and pawn) 18 N×R (not 18 P×B B×B 19 Q×B N×B 20 P×N Q×N winning a piece) 18...N×B 19 P×N B-Q5ch 20 K-R1 B×B 21 Q×B Q×N, with a big advantage to Black; or

(ii) 17 B×P?? B(R3)×N 18 B×N B×B 19 B×Q B×Q, and Black has won a piece.

I have given these examples to illustrate the tactical complexity of the position. Since chess programs are more likely to excel at tactics than they are at strategical planning, it is obviously in their best interests to play sharp variations such as this one. After all, human players are advised to choose opening variations that suit their style, so why should the same advice not hold good for computer programs?

16 ...   N-R4

CPU time: 73 seconds
positions: 84,729
assessment: 20
predicting: 17 B-K3 Q-B3 18 Q-Q2 Q-N3

17   P-R5?

A serious strategic error, since now Black could play 17...P-N4 with a strong Q-side attack. Just as I would advocate storing a list of "good moves" and "good ideas" with each opening variation, I would also suggest storing a list of strategic errors that should be avoided unless there was some substantial tactical justification. The move P-R5 would be high on my list of "bad moves" for positions with this particular Q-side pawn-structure.

White could preserve its advantage with 17 N-K3.

17   ...   N-B5
CPU time: 60 seconds
positions: 69,748
asessment: —30
predicting: 18 P×P P×P 19 B-N3 N-Bch 20 Q×N B×N(B6) 21 P×B N×P 22 R×B N×P.

For the first time in the game CHESS 4.4 (correctly) thinks that it has the advantage. Note that when the main variation involves captures the depth of look-ahead is extended—here it was 10-ply.

18   P×P   P×P
CPU: 65 seconds
positions: 76,015
assessment: —3
predicting: 19 B-Q3 Q-B3 20 Q-B2 N×B 21 Q×N

19   B-K3

On K3 White's bishop is undefended, and this allows the ensuing combination (which, incidentally, is not Black's strongest continuation). 19 N×NP is also bad because of 19...B×N 20 N×R (or 20 B×B

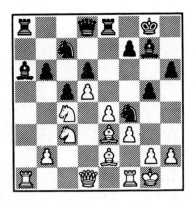

R×B 21 R×R N×R, winning a piece) 20... B×B and 21...B×R winning a piece. In fact White is already lost since there is no satisfactory defence to the threat of 19...N×Bch 20 Q×N P-N4 and 21...P-QN5.

19   ...   B×N(B6)
CPU time: 74 seconds
positions: 85,486
assessment: —47
predicting: 20 P×B B×N 21 B×B R×R 22 Q×R N(2)×P

The text is the beginning of a long combination that is based on the exposed position of White's K3 bishop. Note that the key move of the combination, the capture of White's QP by a black knight, was predicted in a slightly different guise on the previous move.

Considerably stronger than the text however, was 19...N×Bch 20 Q×N P-N4, followed by ...P-QN5 with an easy win. But CHESS 4.4 was using an exhaustive 5-ply search, and for a variation to be examined at a depth greater than 5 it was necessary that the move at depth 6 be a capture (or, in some cases, a check). Since this condition is not satisfied by the continuation 19...N×Bch 20 Q×N P-N4 21 N-R5 P-QN5 22 N-B6, CHESS 4.4 would have no reason to look further and see that 22...B×Q 23 N×Q P×N wins a piece. This sort of oversight could be omitted by widening the restriction on moves considered at depths beyond the exhaustive search level. Instead of considering only captures (and some checks) programs could also consider all checks and direct threats, i.e. moves that attack undefended pieces or pieces of greater value than the attacking piece. This would naturally lead to a slowing down of the search process but in my opinion such a search strategy is an essential part of a good tactical analyser.

20   P×B   B×N
CPU time: 110 seconds
positions: 127,171
assessment: —47
predicting 21 B×B R×R 22 Q×R N(2)×P

Eliminating this knight is an essential part of Black's plan, since it guards the bishop on White's K3. Note that 20...N×Bch 21 Q×N P-N4 22 N-R5 P-QN5 no longer wins material because White can reply 23 P-QB4.

21   B×B   R×R
CPU time: 231 seconds
positions: 340,406
assessment: —38
predicting: 22 Q×R N(B5)×QP 23 B-Q2 N-B3 24 B-Q3 P-Q4

The text is essential so as to decoy the white queen away from her defence of the Q5 square. If 21...N(B5)×QP 22 B×N R×R (or 22...N×B 23 Q×N and Black has lost a piece) 23 B×KBPch, and White has the advantage. Note that even though the depth-5 move in the predicted continuation, 23...N-B3 (remember that 21... R×R is at depth-1), is not a capture or a check, CHESS 4.4 is still searching to a depth of 7-ply. This is because the reduction of material on the board has reduced the average number of branches at each node (the "branching factor") and so a greater depth of search can be conducted within the same time span.

22   Q×R   N(B2)×P?
CPU time: 247 seconds
positions: 364,618
assessment: —25
predicting: 23 B-B1 N-B3 24 B×N P×B 25 R-Q1 Q-B2

The text is inferior to 22...N(B5) ×QP (which CHESS 4.4 was originally intending to play—see the prediction at move 21). The reason that it is inferior is the very continuation predicted by 4.4 itself: 23 B-B1(or Q2) N(Q4) moves 24 B×N P×B, and White has excellent compensation for the pawn in Black's weakened K-side. So although CHESS 4.4 can predict the correct continuation, its assessment of the resulting position is obviously incorrect. This sort of example convinces me that if a chess programmer was presented, by his fairy godmother, with a routine that played perfect tactical chess, he would still be unable to write a really strong chess program because chess is essentially a game of strategy. I would not wish to give the impression that I consider tactics to be unimportant, but I do feel that too much effort has been devoted to tactics and not enough to strategy.

23 B × N(Q5)   N × B
CPU time: 118 seconds
positions: 180,178
assessment: —42
predicting: 24 B × BP N × P 25 B-N4 N-K7ch 26 K-R1 R-K4

A really sophisticated tactical analyser would realise that it is essential to recapture on Q4, simply from the lack of threatening, capturing, and checking alternatives. The greater part of the 118 seconds search time was consumed in the exhaustive part of the search.

24 B × BP   N × P
CPU time: 171 seconds
positions: 243,234
assessment: —27
predicting: 25 B-K3 Q-B2 26 Q-N2 N-R5 27 Q-N5 R-R1

If 24...QP × B 25 R-Q1, picking up the knight.

25 B-N4   N-K7ch
CPU time: 223 seconds
positions: 303,678
assessment: 20
predicting: 26 K-B2 Q-B2 27 R-Q1 (if 27 K × N Q-B5ch and 28...Q × B—D.L.) 27...Q-B5 28 Q-N2 P-N4 29 R × P

CHESS 4.4 is showing bad judgement by predicting 26 K-B2. With queens still on and the position so open, such a move would be very dangerous.

26 K-R1   N-B5
CPU time: 125 seconds
positions: 173,776
assessment: 33
predicting: 27 Q-Q4 N-K3 (otherwise 28 B-B3) 28 Q × QP Q × Q 29 B × Q

Note that with White's queen in the middle of the board (after the predicted 27 Q-Q4) the branching factor increases and the depth of exhaustive search is reduced from 7-ply to 6.

27 R-Q1   Q-R1
CPU time: 96 seconds
positions: 131,952
assessment: 41
predicting: 28 Q-Q4 Q-R5 29 Q × QP Q-B7 30 R-Q2

28 B × P
As CHESS 4.4 had suggested, White would do better to keep the queens on, so as to take advantage of Black's vulnerable K-side.

28 ...   Q × Q
CPU time: 69 seconds
positions: 95,554
assessment: 49
predicting: 29 R × Q R-Q1 30 B × N P × B 31 R-R7

CHESS 4.4's evaluation function is once again proved wrong. The rook ending reached in the predicted line is better for Black because of the passed QNP.

29 R × Q   N-K7
CPU time: 143 seconds
positions: 211,158
assessment: 24
predicting: 30 R-R7 R-QB1 31 P-R3 N-Q5 32 R-N7 R-B3

30 R-QN1   R-QB1
CPU time: 94 seconds

positions: 141,154
assessment: 17
predicting: 31 P-R3 R-B3 32 P-K5 N-B5 33 R-N2 N-Q6

At this point CHESS 4.4 typed out "Be careful", warning its opponent against the trap 31 R × P R-B8 mate.

31 P-R3   **R-B3**
CPU time: 105 seconds
positions: 157,243
assessment: 21
predicting: 32 B-K7 N-B6 33 R-R1 R-B2 34 B-Q6 R-Q2

32 B-K5   **K-R2**
CPU time: 166 seconds
positions: 244,363
assessment: 21
predicting: 33 K-R2 P-B3 34 B-N8 N-B6 35 R-R1 P-N4

33 R-K1   **R-B7**
CPU time: 120 seconds
positions: 181,346
assessment: 17
predicting: 34 R-QN1 R-B4 35 B-Q6 R-B3 36 P-K5 K-N3

34 K-R2   **P-N4**
CPU time: 91 seconds
positions: 135,433
assessment: 16
predicting: 35 R-QN1 R-B4 36 B-Q6 R-B3 37 P-K5 N-B6

35 R-QN1   **R-B4**
CPU time: 211 seconds
positions: 325,677
assessment: 22
predicting: 36 B-Q6 R-B3 37 B-K5 P-B3 38 B-N8 N-B6

It is strange that although CHESS 4.4 assesses the predicted continuation as being in White's favour, it does not try repeating the position

(in its prediction) by 37...R-B4.

36 B-Q6   **R-B3**
CPU time: 193 seconds
positions: 301,748
assessment: 23
predicting: 37 B-N8 N-B6 38 R-N2 R-B5 39 R-Q2 P-KN5

37 B-B8   **R-B7**
CPU time: 120 seconds
positions: 178,803
assessment: 4
predicting: 38 B-Q6 N-Q5 39 K-N1 K-N3 40 B-K5 N-K7

38 R-QR1
Not 38 R × P N-B5 39 R-N6 R × Pch 40 K-R1 P-R4, followed by ...R-N6 and Black will win.

38 ...   **N-B5**
CPU time: 124 seconds
positions: 179,683
assessment: —15
predicting: 39 R-KN1 K-N3 40 B-Q6 K-B3 41 B × N P × B

39 R-KN1   **K-N3**
CPU time: 258 seconds
positions: 373,054
assessment: —11
predicting: 40 B-Q6 R-N7 41 B-K5 R-R7 42 B × N P × B

40 B-N4   **P-B4**
CPU time: 165 seconds
positions: 240,201
assessment: —18
predicting: 41 B-Q6 R-K7 42 B × N P × B 43 R-N1 P × P

41 P × Pch   **K × P**
CPU time: 272 seconds
positions: 408,598
assessment: —17
predicting: 42 B-Q6 P-R4 43 B-R3 R-R7 44 B-Q6 R-K7

42 B-Q6   **R-N7**

CPU time: 234 seconds
positions: 349,264
assessment: —30
predicting: 43 B-R3 R-R7 44 B-N4
P-R4 45 B-Q6 R-Q7

43 K-R1   K-B3?
CPU time: 177 seconds
positions: 259,498
assessment: —23
predicting: 44 B×N P×B 45 R-R1
P-N5 46 R-R7

A human player would recognise that Black's winning chances virtually disappear with the forthcoming exchange, but such conceptual assessments are beyond the capability of programs.

44 B×N   P×B
CPU time: 109 seconds
positions: 181,647
assessment: —27
predicting: 45 R-R1 P-N5 46 R-R6ch
K-N4 47 R-R5ch K-R5 48 R-R7 P-
N6

45 K-R2   P-N5
CPU time: 106 seconds
positions: 169,718
assessment: —19
predicting: 46 R-Q1 P-N6 47 R-Q6ch
K-N4 48 R-Q5ch K-R5 49 R-Q7

46 R-QB1   P-N6
CPU time: 200 seconds
positions: 307,809
assessment: —25
predicting: 47 R-B6ch K-N4 48 R-
QN6 R-N8 49 R-N5ch K-N3 50 R-
N7 P-N7

CHESS 4.4 was now searching to
a depth of 9-ply.

47 R-B6ch   K-N4
CPU time: 148 seconds
positions: 232,952
assessment: 51
predicting: 48 R-B5ch K-N3 49 R-B4
R-QB7 50 R×BP P-N7 51 R-KN4ch
K-B4 53 R-B6 ch

48 R-B5ch   K-N3
CPU time: 197 seconds
positions: 305,443
assessment: 64
predicting: 49 R-B4 K-B4 50 R-B5ch
K-K3 51 R-B6ch K-B4 52 R×RP R-
R7 53 R-R7

10 ply!

49 R-B6ch   K-R4
CPU time: 132 seconds
positions: 211,024
assessment: 61
predicting: 50 R-B5ch K-R5 51 R-B4
R-Q7 52 R×BPch K-N4 53 R-B7 P-
N7

50 R-B5ch   K-N3
CPU time: 111 seconds
positions: 174,421
assessment: 64
*predicting: ***

51 R-B6ch   K-N4
CPU time: 101 seconds
positions: 160,033
assessment: 64
*predicting: ***

52 R-B5ch   K-B3
CPU time: 156
positions: 239,191
assessment: 64
*predicting: ****

53 R-QN5

---

*No prediction in these positions because of a complicated side-effect of CHESS 4.4's transposition table. For the same reason, some later positions have only shallow predictions.

CHAOS refrained from 53 R-B6ch because although it considered Black to have the advantage it did not consider this advantage to be so great as to warrant it playing for a draw. After 53 R-B6ch Black might try 53...K-N2, but after 54 R-B7ch K-B1 (or 54...K-K1 55 R-B8ch K-B2 56 R-B4) 55 R-B4, White picks up the KBP.

The CHAOS programmers might be considered to have been rather unlucky here—had CHAOS' evaluation function calculated Black's advantage to be 0.0002 more than its actual assessment, that score would have been over the threshold beyond which CHAOS *would* have played for a draw!

53   ...   K-N3
CPU time: 89 seconds
positions: 146,942
assessment: —4
predicting: 54 P-R4 R-N8 55 K-R3 P-R4 56 R-N6ch K-B2 57 R-QR6

54   K-N1   R-N8ch
CPU time: 344 seconds
positions: 538,972
assessment: 59

predicting: 55 K-R2 K-B3 56 R-KR5 K-N2 57 R-R4 P-N7 58 R-N4ch K-B3 59 R×Pch K-K4

55   K-R2   K-N2
CPU time: 138 seconds
positions: 212,473
assessment: 60
predicting: 56 R-N6 P-N7 57 P-R4 K-B2 58 R-N4 K-B3 59 R×BPch K-K4

56   R-N4   P-N7
CPU time: 235 seconds
positions: 328,543
assessment: —34
predicting: 57 R-N6 P-R4 58 P-R4 K-B2

57   R-N6   K-B2
CPU time: 116 seconds
positions: 186,533
assessments: —20
predicting: 58 P-R4 P-R4

58   P-R4?
This move is a mistake inasmuch as Black is able to win the KRP by force but although he is then a pawn up, the position should still be a draw with correct play.

58   ...   K-N2
CPU time: 141 seconds
positions: 225,755
assessment: 60
predicting: 59 R-N4 K-N3 60 R-N5 P-R4 61 R-N4 K-B3 62 R×BPch K-K4

59   P-R5   K-B2
CPU time: 136 seconds
positions: 215,660
assessment: —37
predicting: 60 R-N4 K-K3 61 R-N6ch K-K4 62 R-N5ch K-B3 63 R-N7 K-K4

60   R-N8   K-K3

CPU time: 292 seconds
positions: 454,779
assessment: —40
predicting: 61 R-N6ch K-B4 62 R-N5ch K-B3 63 R-N7 K-N4 64 R-N5ch K-R5

From CHESS 4.4's predicted continuation we can see the difficulties facing White. At the end of the predicted variation White is in zugzwang*—if his rook moves off the fifth rank he loses the KRP while if it moves off the QN-file Black wins by 65...R-KR8ch 66 K × R P-N8 = Qch etc. It is this motif of the rook sacrifice that gives Black whatever winning chances there are in this ending.

61 R-N7 K-B4
CPU time: 225 seconds
positions: 354,367
assessment: —33
predicting: 62 R-N5ch K-B3 63 R-N4 K-N4 64 R-N5ch K-R5 65 R-N4 K × P 66 R × BP

So CHESS 4.4 knows that it is winning the KRP.

62 R-N5ch K-B3
CPU time: 87 seconds
positions: 138,706
assessment: —35
predicting: 63 R-N7 K-N4 64 R-N5ch K-R5 65 P-N3 P × Pch 66 K-N2 R-QR8 67 R × P

In this predicted variation, CHESS 4.4 has seen that 66 K × P lost to 66...R-N8ch followed by 67...P-N8 = Q.

63 P-N3??
The losing move. This was probably prompted by the horizon effect: since White is forced to lose a pawn (CHAOS would have seen the fate of its KRP) it prefers to lose the KNP to the KRP since its king is then attacking Black's undefended KNP. The loss of the KRP is pushed over the horizon and CHAOS does not realise that even though the black KNP is attacked, it is never possible for White to play K × P because of the reply...R-N8ch.

Had White kept its rook on the QN-file, Black had only one winning try. This consists of a five stage plan:
(1) Win the KRP as shown above.
(2) Bring the king to QB7. If White plays K-R3 at any stage then ...R-KR8ch allows Black to promote the NP. Also, if White's rook moves off the QN-file without giving check, Black can play ...R-KR8ch.

**zugzwang — A german word used to describe a position in which the player whose turn it is to move loses *because* it is his move.

When Black's king is on QB7 Black threatens to move the rook to QB8 followed by ...K-N8, ...R-B7, ...K-B8 and P-N8 = Q. So as soon as Black plays ...K-QB7, White must give check with his rook on the QB-file to drive Black's king away from the protection of the NP. White then returns with his rook to the QN-file and Black cannot move his rook because the NP will be *en prise.*

(3) Black marches his king from QB7 to KB7.

(4) Black advances his KRP to R6, forcing White to play P×P. It is vital however, that Black plays the move ...P-R6 when White's rook is not on QN3, protecting the KBP.

(5) After White has played P×P, Black replies ...K×P, and if White then plays P-R4 he is lost after K-N5. In any case White cannot prevent the advance of the KBP.

The reason that this plan fails is that White can play R-QN3 in reply to Black's K-KB7, so that after P-R6; P×P, Black cannot pick up the white KBP. Whether CHAOS would have found this defence or whether it would have overlooked the full force of the threat ...P-R6, I do not know.

Incidentally, I asked David Slate to see what his program would have done had CHAOS not played 63 P-N3. "Surprisingly, the program found most of the winning try, winning the king rook pawn, getting its king to K7 (*not* KB7), and then playing ...P-R6! However, playing White, I refused to play P×P. Black

played immediately ...P×P, I recaptured K×P and the game was drawn,"

63   ...   P × Pch
CPU time: 95 seconds
positions: 151,156
assessment: —134
predicting: 64 K-N2 K-K3 65 R-N3 K-B4 66 R-N5ch K-B5 67 R-N7 K-N4 68 K×P K×P

An 11-ply prediction! When capturing the KNP CHESS 4.4 typed out "That was easy".

64   K-N2   K-K3
CPU time: 183 seconds
positions: 309,719
assessment: —134
predicting: 65 5-N3 K-B4 66 R-N4 K-N4 67 R-N6ch K-R5 68 R-N7 K×P 69 K×P

65   R-N3   K-B4
CPU time: 215 seconds
positions: 361,557
assessment: —134
predicting: 66 R-N5ch K-B5 67 R-N4ch K-N4 68 R-N5ch K-R5 69 R-N7 K×P 70 K×P

If CHESS 4.4 considered checks (as well as captures) beyond its exhaustive search depth, it would realise that White's last move in its predicted variation is a loser.

66   R-N6   K-N4
CPU time: 228 seconds
positions: 360,169
evaluation: —151
predicting: 67 R-N3 K×P 68 R-N6 K-N4 69 R-N5ch K-B3 70 R-N6ch K-K4 71 R×RP

67   R-N5ch   K-R5
CPU time: 136 seconds
positions: 212,588

assessment: —151

predicting: 68 R-N7 K×P 69 R-N6 K-N4 70 R-N5ch K-B3 71 R-N6ch K-K4 72 R×RP

68   R-N8   K×P

CPU time: 90 seconds

positions: 138,265

assessment: —154

predicting: 69 R-N5ch K-N3 70 R-N6ch

   "That was easy."

69   R-N5ch   K-N3

CPU time: 94 seconds

positions: 148,694

assessment: —161

predicting: 70 R-N6ch K-B4 71 R-N5ch K-K3 72 R-N6ch K-Q4 73 P-B4 R-QR8 74 R×NP

70   R-N6ch   K-B4

CPU time: 97 seconds

positions: 150,410

assessment: —159

predicting: 71 R-N5ch K-K3 72 R-N6ch K-Q4 73 R-N5ch

71   R-N5ch   K-K3

CPU time: 143 seconds

positions: 217,260

assessment: —168

predicting: 72 R-N6ch K-Q4 73 R-N5ch K-Q5 74 R-N7 K-K6 75 R-N4 P-R4 76 K×P

72   R-N6ch   K-Q4

CPU time: 239 seconds

positions: 372,605

assessment: —275

predicting: 73 R-N5ch K-B3 74 R-N3 P-R4 75 K×P R-N8ch 76 K-R4 P-N8=Q 77 R×Q R×R 78 K×P

   12-ply!

   "Be careful."

73   R-N5ch   K-B3

CPU time: 195 seconds

positions: 302,090

assessment: —275

predicting: 74 R-N3 P-R4 75 K×P R-N8ch 76 K-R4 P-N8=Q 77 R×Q R×R 78 K×P.

   "Be careful."

74   R-N3   P-R4

CPU time: 172 seconds

positions: 288,717

assessment: —276

predicting: 75 K×P R-N8ch 76 K-R4 P-N8=Q 77 R×Q R×R 78 K×P K-B4

   "Be careful."

75   P-B4   P-R5

CPU time: 170 seconds

positions: 286,037

assessment: —282

predicting: 76 P-B5 K-Q4 77 P-B6 K-K3 78 R-N6ch K-B2 79 R-N4 K×P 80 R×RP

76   R-N8

76   ...   K-Q4

CPU time: 101 seconds

positions: 170,279

assessment: —364

predicting: 77 R-N4 K-K3 78 R-N5 K-B3 79 R-N7 K-B4 80 K-R3

Of course Black can win by playing 76...P-R6ch 77 K×RP R-KR8ch 78 K×P P-N8=Q, but CHESS 4.4 must have realised that with its king defending its KNP (from KN5 or KB5) it could reach a similar position with an extra pawn (the KNP). In fact with the black king on KN5 there is the threat of mate by ...P-R5.

77   R-N5ch   K-K5
CPU time: 199 seconds
positions: 351,300
assessment: —538
predicting: 78 P-B5 K-B5 79 P-B6 P-R6ch 80 K×P R-KR8ch 81 K-N2 P-N8=Q 82 R×Q R×R
"Be careful."

78   R-N6   K-B4
CPU time: 161 seconds
positions: 297,277
assessments: —541
predicting: 79 R-N5ch K-N5 80 R-N5ch K×P 81 R-N4ch K-B4 82 R-N4 K-N4

79   R-N5ch   K-N5
CPU time: 141 seconds
positions: 268,418
assessment: —538
predicting: 80 R-N5ch K×P 81 R-N4ch K-K6 82 R-N4 K-Q6 83 R-N5 K-K7 84 R-K5ch K-Q7

80   R-N5ch
"Oh, you had that."

80   ...   K×P
CPU time: 12 seconds
positions: 36
assessment: —299
predicting: 81 R-N4ch K-K6 82 R×RP

81   R-N4ch   K-K6
CPU time: 203 seconds

positions: 381,628
assessment: —531
predicting: 82 R-N4 K-Q6 83 R-N8 K-B7 84 R-QB8ch K-Q7 85 R-Q8ch K-K7 86 R-K8ch K-Q6

82   R-N4   K-Q6
CPU time: 196 seconds
positions: 357,893
assessment: —533
predicting: 83 R-N7 K-Q5 84 R-N3 K-B5 85 R-N6 K-B6 86 R-QB6ch K-Q7
"Be careful."

83   R-N5   K-B6
CPU time: 99 seconds
positions: 179,205
assessment: —529
predicting: 84 R-N8 K-B7 85 R-QB8ch K-Q7 86 R-Q8ch K-K7 87 R-K8ch K-Q8

84   R-QB5ch   K-N5
CPU time: 201 seconds
positions: 372,503
assessment: —680
predicting: 85 R-B7 R-N8ch 86 K-R3 R-KR8ch 87 K-N4 P-N8=Q 88 R-QN7ch K-B5 89 R×Q R×R 90 K×P
12-ply!!
"Be careful."

85   R-B6   R-N8ch
CPU time: 148 seconds
positions: 265,377
assessment: —1009
predicting: 86 K-R3 K-R4 87 K×P P-N8=Q 88 R-B5ch K-N5 89 R-KN5 Q-K5ch 90 K-R5

86   K-R3
"Oh, you had that."

86   ...   R-KR8ch
CPU time: 138 seconds
positions: 252,691

assessment: —987
predicting: 87 K-N4 P-N7 88 R-QN6ch K-B5 89 R×P P-N8=Qch 90 K-B5

The text is certainly the most accurate but it is rather greedy. After 86...P-N8=Q 87 R-QN6ch K moves 88 R×Q R×R 89 K×P. Black is "only" a rook and a pawn ahead. After the text however, Black's material advantage is greater.

87 K-N2

"Oh, you had that."

87 ...   **K-R4!!**

CPU time: 173 seconds
positions: 307,636
assessment: —1013
predicting: 88 R-B5ch K-N3 89 R-B8 R-R7ch 90 K-B3 R-KB7ch 91 K-N4 P-N8=Q 92 K×P

If 87...P-N8=Q 88 R-QN6ch K moves 80 R×Q R×R and this time Black is "only" a rook and two pawns ahead. But by moving his king off the QN-file, Black ensures himself an even greater advantage: If now 88 K×R P-N8=Qch 89 K-N2 Q-K5ch and 90...Q×R

88 R-B5ch   **K-R3**

CPU time: 120 seconds
positions: 206,274
assessment: —1179
predicting: 89 R-B6ch K-N2 90 R-KN6 P-N8=Q 91 R-N7ch K-B3 92 K-B3 R-KN8

89 R-B6ch   **K-N2**

CPU time: 170 seconds
positions: 286,919
assessment: —1175
predicting: 90 R-B6 P-N8=Q 91 R-B7ch K-N3 92 R-B6ch K-B4 93 K-B4 Q-K8

"Be careful."

90 R-K6   **P-N8=Q**

"That was easy."

CHESS 4.4's greed has at last been justified—it has promoted a pawn and kept all of its material. The remainder of the game is of no interest.

91	R-K7ch	K-B3
92	K-B3	Q-B4ch
93	K-K2	P-N7

And CHAOS' programmers resigned their program.

The following year, 1976, the Northwestern program decided that the time had come to show human tournament players what it could do. It entered the class B section at the annual Paul Masson tournament in Saratoga, California, and just to ensure that the humans did not have any cause for complaint it was decided in advance that the program would not claim any prize money that it might win. The program, by now CHESS 4.5, was running on a CDC Cyber 176.

The result of the tournament was a win for CHESS 4.5, which achieved a performance rating of 2184 (i.e. high U.S. Expert). The program's games were not really of the caliber of a 2184 player but showed quite clearly that its unsuccessful opponents were psyched out, playing moves that they would not have chosen against a strong human opponent. I have noticed this syndrome quite often when watching humans battling against computer programs; most people whom I have quizzed about their computer games confessed to feeling unnerved in competition with a non-human adversary. Others have simply underestimated the strength of the program. Herein lies a whole new area of psychology - the study of human reactions to intellectual encounters with computers.

The most impressive result achieved by CHESS 4.5 in Saratoga was a win in an exhibition game played against an A-player (rating 1886). This game was played at a fast time limit (30 moves in 30 minutes), a factor which helps the program for reasons explained in chapter 3 on blitz play.

White: A. Hough
Black: CHESS 4.5

Modern Benoni

1	P-Q4	N-KB3
2	P-QB4	P-B4
3	P-Q5	P-K3

This might be called the program's favourite weapon. It has won some fine games with this defence.

4	N-QB3	P×P
5	P×P	P-Q3
6	N-B3	P-KN3
7	P-KN3	B-N2
8	B-N2	0-0
9	0-0	B-N5
10	N-Q2	Q-K2
11	P-KR3	B-Q2

Now Black threatens ...P-QN4, a thematic move in the Modern Benoni.

12	P-QR4	N-R3
13	N-B4	N-K1
14	Q-N3	N-N5
15	B-B4	P-KN4

A difficult move to assess. On the one hand it weakens Black's K-side, but it does have the advantage of driving away the KB4 bishop before White can play N-K4.

16	B-Q2	P-KR3
17	K-R2	N-B2
18	P-R5	P-B4

Black should continue with 18...N-N4; the text is too loosening. But it is not yet possible for programs to consider long term positional ideas, and so a move which is overtly aggressive will often be made even though it is not sound.

19	P-B4	QR-N1

19...N-N4 is essential.

20	P-K4	
20	...	BP×P

Forced - White threatened 21 P-K5.

21	N×KP	

Black's position is hopeless.

21	...	N(5)×P

22	P × P	Q-K3
23	N(K4) × QP	

Why not capture on KR6?

23	...	P × P
24	QR-K1	Q-N3

25 N-K3

Mistakenly going into complications in time-trouble.

25	...	Q × N
26	N × N	B-K3
27	R × B	N × R
28	R-K1	R-B7

Presumably White overlooked this move. Now that the KN2 bishop is pinned White does not have the combination based on R × N followed by N-K7ch and B-Q5.

29	R × N	Q × R

White lost on time

In any case White is lost. If 30 N-K7ch or 30 N-B6ch, Black can reply 30...K-B2.

The Northwestern program's next real test came in February 1977 when it entered the Minnesota Open Championship. David Slate and Larry Atkin expected their 'baby' to score 2-4 and thought that 3-3 would be a real success. CHESS 4.5 surprised everyone by scoring 5-1 and taking the title on tie-break. Once again I felt that some of the 'blame' for its victory must be attributed to the fallible psyche of its opponents, as seen from the following game.

White: CHESS 4.5
Black: Fenner (2016)

Sicilian Defence

1	P-K4	P-QB4
2	N-KB3	P-K3
3	P-Q4	P × P
4	N × P	P-QR3
5	P-QB4	N-KB3
6	B-Q3	Q-B2
7	0-0	B-B4
8	N-N3	B-R2
9	N-B3	N-B3
10	B-N5!	

Taking advantage of the vulnerability of Black's K-side caused by manoeuvering his bishop over to QR2.

10	...	N-K4
11	B × N	P × B

Now Black cannot very well castle K-side.

| 12 | Q-K2 | P-Q3 |

13   K-R1

Preparing P-B4.

13 ...	B-Q2
14 P-B4	N × B
15 Q × N	0-0-0
16 QR-Q1	B-B3
17 P-KB5	

Hereabouts White's play is rather aimless. It would have been better to put a rook on QB1 and to launch some sort of attack on the Q-side.

17 ...	B-N1
18 P-N3	P-KR4?!
19 P × P	P-R5
20 R × P	RP × P
21 Q × NP	QR-N1?

After 21...P × P or 21...P-Q4, the situation would be quite unclear.

22   P × P!

| 22   ... | Q × P |

If 22...R × Q 23 P-B8 = Qch R × Q 24 R × Rch K-Q2 25 R-B7ch and 26 R × Q, winning material.

| 23   R × Q | R × Q |
| 24   N-Q5 | |

At this point Fenner offered a draw which the program declined.

24 ...	B-K1
25 N-N6ch	K-Q1
26 R × NP	B-B3
27 R × Bch	K-B2
28 R-QB8ch!	

Presumably Black had overlooked this move. If 28 R × R??? B × P is mate.

| 28   ... | R × R |

If 28...K-N2 29 R × B K × R 30 N-Q5, with an easy endgame win.

The authors, Monroe Newborn (foreground) and David Levy (rear left), discuss a game with Ben Mittman, director of the Vogelbach Computer Center at Northwestern University and coach of the world champion programmers (rear right).

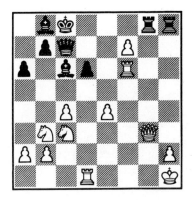

29 P×R   B×Pch

30   K-N1   R-KR1?

Hoping for a swindle, 30...K×N 31 R×Pch would have been hopeless, objectively, but at least the program would be forced to play an endgame where it was not a piece ahead.

31   N-Q5ch   K-B3
32   N-R5ch   Resigns

If 32...K-B4 33 P-N4 mate or 33...K-Q2 34 N-KB6ch and 35 N×B.

During the remainder of 1977 the program hit the headlines again quite a few times. Its victory in the Minnesota Open qualified it for a place in the state's closed championship the following weekend but there it did not fare so well - its opponents were prepared for it and the program finished in last place with one win, one draw and three losses. A few weeks later it gave a simultaneous exhibition in New York against ten human opponents, including Edward Lasker, Walter Goldwater (President of the Marshall Chess Club) and Burt Hochberg (Editor of *Chess Life and Review*). CHESS 4.5 scored eight wins, one draw and only one loss. In September it competed in the Aronson Open in London, over an open telephone line from Arden Hills, Minnesota where the Cyber computer is located. In this event it achieved a tournament rating of 2000 with a score of 3$^{1}/_{2}$ out of 6. One of its draws was against the captain of the England junior team who had expressed some contempt for the program before the game but who found himself unable to win a rook ending against it despite having an extra pawn. At the end of the year it gave another exhibition, this time in Paris, against such notables as Monsieur Chandon Moet (of the champagne family) and Roger Vadim, but from the publicity surrounding the event it was clear that the program, not its human opponents, was the celebrity.

The fame of the Northwestern program is quite justifiable. It is already stronger than more than 99% of serious chess players (by serious I mean anyone who finds it worthwhile to join their national federation or subscribe to a chess magazine) and it can accomplish great feats at blitz chess (see chapter 3). What then are its limitations and how likely is it that Slate and Atkin will find some way to surmount them and make a quantum leap forward during the next few years?

Reprinted courtesy of Minnesota State Chess Association, The Minnesota Chess Journal, *Vol. 14, No. 2.*

One of the biggest problems still faced by chess programmers is how to develop an evaluation function which performs well in quiet positions. Examples of this failing can be seen in the notes to my games with CHESS 4.5 where the program often thought that it had an advantage when in fact it was quite lost. Another illustration of incorrect evaluation can be seen in the game between CHAOS and CHESS 4.4 (page **32**). On move 22 CHESS 4.4 made a capture which should have given its opponent a positional advantage (with correct play) - obviously CHESS 4.4 thought that after White's best continuation, 23 B-B1 N(Q4) moves 24 B×N P×B, the position was still good for Black.

It does not matter how far you look if you cannot see properly and it does not matter how deeply your program searches if it cannot make an accurate evaluation of the positions at the end of its search. This is why the human is, at the moment, the master of the machine. The human sees relatively little but understands a lot, while the best chess programs see 10,000-50,000 times more but do not understand what they see. I maintain that this blind, brute force approach produces a kind of monkey/typewriter situation in which a program appears to play moderately well whereas it is actually playing very weak chess so many times that its best results resemble the moves of strong players. Some programmers, e.g. Slate and Newborn, my co-author, argue that as the search becomes deeper strategy and tactics merge into one, but in my opinion this view is erroneous.

Let us now look at two further examples.

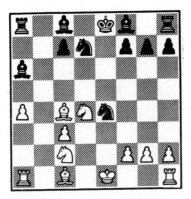

This position is from the game Perry (White) v CHESS 4.6, played in the Aronson Open Tournament in London, September 1977. CHESS 4.4 (to move) continued:

13	...	N-K4?
14	B-Q5	N-Q6ch
15	K-B1	N(K5) × KBP
16	B × R	N × R

It is not difficult to see that the Black knight on KR8 is trapped. Why did the program follow this continuation? Because when playing 13...N-K4? it would have analyzed the whole of the tactical continuation which was actually played and it would have noticed that 17 K-N1 allows the knight to escape from the corner. It would not, however, have examined the move 17 B-K3 because that is a non-tactical move, i.e. it is not a capture or a check or even a direct threat. The program looks at the "quiescent" position in the above diagram and assesses it as being good for Black who is a pawn up.

Perry naturally played 17 B-K3, trapping the knight in the corner, and eventually he won the game. An average human player with only a moderate conceptual ability can see at a glance, without so much as a 1-ply search, that after 17 B-K3 the capture of the knight on KR1 is inevitable - it can never escape. But how does one explain the concept of "never" to a chess program?

The next position is not taken from a game but is based on a well known idea in the Dragon Variation of the Sicilian Defence.

White is a queen up for a knight and three pawns, an overwhelming material advantage under normal circumstances. Yet Black has a clearly won position because although White's queen is not attacked and may not be attacked (Black's knight can not move without allowing the queen to escape) the queen will never get out of its cage. A brute force program might well see that the queen will not escape during the next 10 or 20 ply, but it will not be able to analyze as far as "never"! Furthermore, if White plays the best moves it will be another 14 ply before Black's win is evident to the program: *1 K-N2 P-K4 2 K-B3 P-R4 3 K-B4 P-R5 4 K-N4 P-K5 5 K × P P-K6 6 K-N3* (say) **P-K7 7 K** moves **P-K8 = Q.** If CHESS 4.6 were to reach the diagrammed position at the end of a branch of analysis it would undoubtedly consider the position to be quiescent (which it is) and evaluate it as winning for White (which it is not). It would not see the need to analyze what might happen after another 14 ply. Yet to any average (human) club player the diagrammed position is an obvious win for Black.

If I am correct in assuming that brute force programming will never produce a World Champion, it becomes necessary to question whether or not computer programs will be able to play real chess by other means. If they are constrained to look at trees that are more human in size (50-100 nodes), instead of the monster (1 million - 3 million node) trees examined at present, perhaps the CPU time saved can be used to examine each terminal node with a much better "understanding" (i.e. a more sophisticated evaluation mechanism) than is employed at the moment. This small tree approach has already been shown to produce moderately reasonable results, such as Marsland's WITA (recently renamed AWIT) and Richter's SCHACH MV5.6. Consider, for example, the following game.

White: SCHACH MV5.6
Black: Fischer/Schneider
1st German Computer Tournament
Dortmund 1975
Irregular Opening

1	N-QB3	P-Q4
2	P-Q4	B-N5
3	P-B3	B-B4
4	P-K4	P×P
5	P×P	B-Q2
6	N-B3	

So far White's play has been perfectly logical and he has taken command of the centre.

6	...	N-QB3
7	P-K5	P-K3
8	B-KN5	B-K2
9	Q-Q2	P-KN3
10	B-Q3	P-N3
11	B×B	KN×B
12	0-0-0	

Continuing sensibly, completing his development and preparing for an attack against Black's K-side.

12	...	0-0
13	Q-R6	

With the terrible threat of 14 N-KN5.

13	...	N-B4
14	B×N	NP×B
15	N-KN5	Q×Nch

Otherwise it's mate.

16	Q×Qch	K-R1
17	P-KN4	

Opening up another line of attack.

17	...	P×P
18	Q×NP	P-B4
19	Q-R4	P-B5
20	N-K4	

Now the other knight joins in the attack.

20	...	P-B6
21	N-N5	R-B2
22	N×Rch	K-N1
23	Q-B6	P-B7
24	N-R6 mate	

White's play is rather crude but it definitely looks as though SCHACH had a plan - to attack the enemy king. Yet SCHACH was playing *without any look-ahead whatsoever!!*

WITA (or AWIT) has competed in a number of computer chess tournaments. Typically, the programs that finish behind it or level with it in these events look at two orders of magnitude times as many positions as WITA when making each move. This, to some extent, confirms the view that it is not only what one looks at that is important but also what one sees.

Having attacked the brute force approach and praised the small tree search we shall now examine some of the problems that will face even those programmers who follow the second path. These problems relate to the assessment of positions that are encountered as terminal nodes on the game tree.

The position in Diagram 3 has already been shown to present evaluation difficulties. Consider now the same position but with Black's pawn removed from K2 and placed on Q2.

This position is a win for *White* because the White king can stop both pawns no matter whose turn it is to move. e.g. **1 K-N2 P-Q4 2 K-N3 P-R4 3 K-R4 P-Q5 4 K-N3,** and now both **4...P-Q6 5 K-B3 P-R5 6 K×P P-R6 7 K-B2 P-R7 8 K-N2** and **4...P-R5ch 5 K×P P-Q6 6 K-N3 P-Q7 7 K-B2,** win for White, because once the pawns have been captured Black must move either his king or his knight, allowing the White queen to become active.

The small difference in position (in comparison with the material situation) between this example and the position in the previous diagram changes a win for Black into a win for White. In order for a program to be able to cope with this delicate a difference it must have an enormous amount of chess knowledge. Here, for example, it would be necessary for a program to know that a lone king cannot stop two unaided passed pawns if they are separated by three empty files but that the king *can* stop the pawns when they are separated by only two files.

Let us next turn to the problem of *zugzwang*. This term describes a situation in which the side whose turn it is to move is at a disadvantage because of and only because of the fact that it is his turn to move. A simple example can be seen in the following diagram.

If it is White to move he is in *zugzwang*. 1 K-K6 is stalemate while any other move allows 1...K×P with an immediate draw. If it is Black to move then he is in *zugzwang* - he must move off K1 and then White plays K-Q7 followed by P-K8 = Q.

The concept of *zugzwang* is fundamental to a large proportion of endgame theory and many endgames are decided only because of a *zugzwang* possibility. But how is a program to recognize that a position is *zugzwang* when evaluating that position as a terminal node on the game tree? Any static evaluation mechanism must take into account whose turn it is to move, but it is totally alien to the very idea of static evaluation that there can exist positions in which possession of the move constitutes a disadvantage. *Zugzwang* positions, when encountered as terminal nodes, will therefore be assessed wrongly, often leading to disastrous results.

It is not only *zugzwang* positions themselves that can cause problems. Positions that will eventually lead to *zugzwang* can also give rise to incorrect assessments.

White to play draws by **1 K-N2 K-Q1 2 K-B2 K-K2 3 K-Q2 K-B2 4 K-K2 K-N3 5 K-B3 K-R4 6 K-N3**, followed by K-R3-N3-R3 ad infinitum. But with Black to move White loses because the Black king can reach KN5 and

White will then be in *zugzwang*, forced to move away from his defence of the KBP. When encountering the diagrammed position as a terminal node how can a program be expected to realize the *zugzwang* possibility that exists 15-ply further on?

Conclusion

Chess is an extremely complex game in which subtle nuances abound. Brute force methods are clearly inadequate for the task of dealing with subtlety and even the search of small trees, although allowing more time for the evaluation of terminal nodes, does not solve the problem of the inability of programs to conceptualize. Until Artifical Intelligence makes giant strides in the realm of concept formation it will be impossible for chess programs to exhibit the understanding of a Fischer. Until that time they must content themselves with being able to play a particular form of chess very, very well but at the same time admit that they do not play real chess.

With its present level of intelligence and a very fast typewriter the monkey can type innumerable crude sonnets, but without increasing its I.Q. it will never write Hamlet.

With their present level of sophistication, and running on very fast computers, the best chess programs can play innumerable crude games, but without increasing their 'understanding' of chess they will never play with the subtlety of a World Champion.

3 Blitz Play

The term "blitz play" in chess is used to describe a game played at high speed. Instead of moving at an average of from 2 to $3^3/_4$ minutes per move, the players must make all of their moves within a short period of time - usually five minutes. Alternatively, the players are required to move every five or ten seconds.

Blitz chess does not allow the players the luxury of long term planning. Moves are made by instinct, with little or no calculation to back it up. Since strategical planning is denied the players the game is normally highly tactical in nature. Sacrifices are more common than in normal chess because although they are mostly theoretically unsound they are not easy to refute given the time restriction.

Because of their ability to calculate tactical variations with considerable accuracy and to a great depth, the strongest chess programs are very adept blitz players. They will not leave material *en prise* but they will grab any tactical opportunity which presents itself. The only way for a human opponent to outwit a strong program is to avoid all tactics except when they are essential or definitely advantageous. In the game which follows, the human player (an International Grandmaster) outplays the program positionally but then makes the mistake of trying to win by tactical means. As a result he became the first Grandmaster ever to lose to a computer program.

Since programs are not yet linked to robots which can move the pieces for them and punch the button on the chess clock, special rules are used for human v comptuer blitz play. The human uses a chess clock and makes all his moves in five minutes in the normal way. The program is constrained to move at an average rate of five seconds per move and if it has not given mate or announced mate by move sixty (i.e. when it has consumed five minutes of C.P.U. time) then it loses on time.

White: CHESS 4.6
Black: Michael Stean

London, September 1977
Owen's Defence

1	P-K4	P-QN3

Designed to get the program out of its openings book.

2	P-Q4	B-N2
3	N-QB3	P-QB4
4	P×P	

A positional error, leaving Black with more pawns controlling the centre and opening up the QN-file along which Black will eventually be able to counter-attack.

4	...	P×P
5	B-K3	P-Q3
6	B-QN5ch	N-Q2
7	N-B3	P-K3
8	0-0	

White has a big lead in developing but Black's pawns control the centre.

8	...	P-QR3
9	B × Nch	Q × B
10	Q-Q3	N-K2
11	QR-Q1	R-Q1
12	Q-B4	

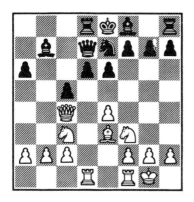

"Threatening" 13 B × P, since the recapture 13...P × B would leave Black's queen *en prise* to White's rook, but in fact Black can meet 13 B × P with 13...Q-B3, winning a piece.

12	...	N-N3
13	KR-K1	B-K2
14	Q-N3	Q-B3
15	K-R1?!	

A strange move, putting its king on a diagonal dominated by its opponent's queen and bishop. The reason was probably that CHESS 4.6 considered its other pieces to be on their optimal squares and so it decided to move its king as far away from the centre as possible in order that it might be safer.

| 15 | ... | 0-0 |
| 16 | B-N5 | B-R1 |

17	B × B	N × B
18	P-QR4	R-N1
19	Q-R2	R-N5
20	P-QN3	

Overprotecting the QRP and the QNP, but shutting the queen even further out of play.

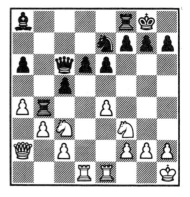

Let us now survey the scene. Black's pawns still dominate the centre, controlling the squares ...Q5, ...Q4, and ...K4, while White's KP attacks only one central square. Black's queen and bishop exert pressure along an important diagonal and his QN5 rook is actively placed. In contrast, White's queen is out of play and he has no active possibilities at his disposal. It is therefore quite reasonable to conclude that Black has a marked positional advantage - in a game between two Grandmasters, with no time shortage, I would expect Black to win every time.

Stean decided that his positional advantage was so overwhelming that the time had come for a tactical assault on White's king along the diagonal. In the ensuing complica-

tions he discovers, to his horror,
that the program can sometimes calculate better than a Grandmaster.

20 ...   P-B4?!

Attempting to open up the diagonal. 20...P-Q4 was a better way of
going about it, and if 21 N-K5 Q-N2
22 N-Q3 R-Q5 23 N × BP R × R 24
R × R Q-B3, followed by 25...P × P.

21 N-KN5   P × P

22 N(B3) × P!

Not 22 N × P(K6) because of
22...R × BP, with a strong attack
against the white king.

22 ...   R × P

At first sight this move looks
strong, since 23 N × R loses at once
to 23...Q × NP mate. But CHESS
4.6 has seen further than its opponent and now plays

23 R × P!

"Bloody iron monster" exclaimed
the Grandmaster, who only now
realised that his queen is needed to
prevent R-Q8 mate. Since it is impossible for the Black queen to
defend ...Q1 and remain on the
crucial diagonal, Black must lose
material.

23 ...   Q × R

The best try.

24 N × Q   R × NP

Now Black is threatening
25...R × Ndis ch, 25...R × BPdis ch
(winning the queen) and 25...R-
K7dis ch (winning the rook), but
CHESS 4.6 had seen this position
coming and had everything under
control.

25 N(N5)-K4!

Blocking the diagonal. CHESS
4.6 had already "seen" this move

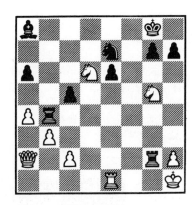

when playing its 21st move!

25 ...   R-N5

Apparently winning a piece, since
the K4 knight cannot move and
cannot be defended again.

26 P-B4!

Cutting the ...QN5 rook off from
its attack on the knight.

26 ...   N-B4

So that if 27 N × N P × N, winning
the other knight which is pinned
against the White king by the
bishop.

27 P-R3

"This computer is a genius" -
Stean.

27 ...   N-N6ch

28 K-R2   R × N

29 Q-KB2!

Yet another tactical blow. Stean
had only expected 29 N × R N × N
when Black has two minor pieces
and a pawn for the queen, but
CHESS 4.6 finds a mate threat (30
Q-B7ch K-R1 31 Q-B8mate) which
forces an even greater material
advantage.

29 ...   P-R3

30	N × R	N × N
31	Q-B3	

Winning two pieces for the rook and emerging with queen against rook and pawn.

31	...	R-N1
32	R × N	R-KB1
33	Q-N4	B × R

34	Q × KPch	K-R1
35	Q × B	R-B3
36	Q-K5	R-QN3
37	Q × BP	R × P
38	Q-QB8ch	K-R2
39	Q × P	Resigns

Stean was in no doubt that the program would be able to promote a pawn and force mate by move 60.

David Slate, of CHESS 4.6, records a move.

CHESS 4.6's win against Stean was no fluke. During 1977 it won a number of other games against players holding the title of International Master, including myself, Berliner (former World Correspondence Champion), Day and Vranesic, and it won one game against International Grandmaster Robert Hubner, rated amongst the top dozen players in the world. At the end of 1977 I estimated its ability at blitz chess to be in the range 2300-2400. This, in itself, is a great achievement, which appeared most unlikely a decade ago.

In the remainder of this chapter I shall comment on four more of this program's blitz victories played during 1977. Each of its opponents is an International Master.

White: CHESS 4.6
Black: Hans Berliner

Pittsburgh, March 1977
Bird's Opening

1	P-KB4	P-KN3
2	N-QB3	B-N2
3	P-K4	P-QB4

Transposing into a Sicilian Defence.

4	N-B3	N-QB3
5	B-B4	P-K3
6	0-0	KN-K2
7	P-K5	

Otherwise Black plays 7...P-Q4, with advantage.

7	...	P-Q3
8	N-K4	

The tactics are already beginning. If 8...P-Q4 9 N-Q6ch K-B1 10 B-N5, and Black's king is awkwardly placed.

8	...	P×P
9	P×P	N×P
10	B-N5ch	N(K2)-B3
11	P-Q3	0-0
12	N×N	N×N
13	B-K3	

White has some pressure for the pawn, but objectively speaking this should not be enough.

13	...	P-QR3
14	B-R4	P-QN4
15	B×NP!?	

Complicating the position still fur-

ther, but at the cost of a piece.

15	...	P×B
16	B×P	R-K1
17	P-Q4	N-B3
18	P-B3	P-K4

18...Q-B2 should have led to an easy win, since 19 N-Q6 R-Q1 gives White nothing. I imagine that in this position Black was confident of victory no matter what he played - after all, he is a piece up.

19	N-Q6	P×P

If 19...R-K3 20 Q-B3, attacking QB6 and KB7.

20	Q-B3	

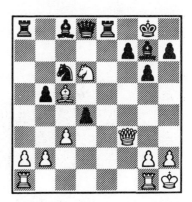

20	...	N-K4??

Admitting defeat. Black had to play 20...B-Q2.

21	Q×R	P-Q6
22	N×R	Q×N
23	P-QR4	P-R4

24	P×P	N-N5
25	R-R7	Q-K4

One last try.

26	Q×Bch	K-R2
27	Q-B7	Q-K7
28	Q×P	Resigns

White: CHESS 4.6
Black: Lawrence Day

Toronto, August 1977
Sicilian Defence

1	P-K4	P-QB4
2	N-KB3	N-QB3
3	B-N5	P-Q3
4	0-0	B-Q2
5	P-B3	N-B3
6	R-K1	P-QR3
7	B-R4	P-QN4
8	B-B2	B-N5
9	P-KR3	B×N
10	Q×B	

White is handling the opening rather well, considering that it is not a tactical system.

10	...	P-KN3
11	P-Q3	B-N2
12	B-B4	

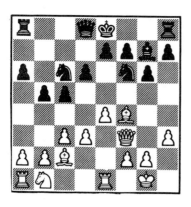

12	...	N-Q2
13	N-Q2	0-0

14   B-QN3

Not a bad move but a negative one, illustrating the program's inability to form a concrete plan.

14	...	R-B1
15	P-QR4	N(B3)-K4
16	Q-K2	Q-N3
17	P×P	P×P
18	B-K3	N-QB3

Black was afraid of 19 P-KB4.

19	N-B3	Q-N2
20	N-N5	N(B3)-K4
21	P-KB4	

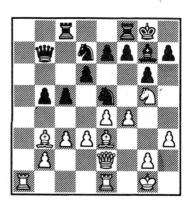

21	...	P-B5

Once again the human goes in for tactics, but he has overlooked White's strong reply.

22   R-R7!

Now White begins to take complete command of the situation.

22	...	Q-B3
23	P×N	P×B
24	P-Q4!	P-Q4

The point of White's previous move is that 24...P×P loses to 25 P-Q5 Q-B5 26 Q×Q and 27 R×N, when White has an extra piece.

25	P×P	Q×QP
26	R(1)-R1	P-B3

27	P×P	P×P
28	Q-N4!	

A strong tactical blow, threatening to complete White's control of the seventh rank.

28	...	P-B4
29	Q-B3	Q×Q
30	N×Q	

White does not yet have any advantage in material but its positional plus is of decisive proportions. With a rook on the seventh rank, complete domination of the QR-file and the possibility of attacking Black's weak, doubled QNPs, CHESS 4.6 has a winning position.

A few years ago the best chess programs would not be able to win this position against a strong human opponent. Here, however, CHESS 4.6 exhibits excellent technique in converting its positional advantage into the full point.

30	...	N-B3
31	R(1)-R3	N-Q4
32	B-B2	P-N5!

The best chance, but not good enough.

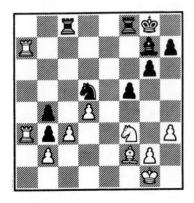

33	R×P	

Not 33 P×P R-B8ch 34 K-R2 R-B7, attacking the bishop, followed by 35...R×QNP, ...R-N8 and ...P-N7, when Black might win.

33	...	P×P
34	R(3)-N7!	B-R3
35	P×P	R×P
36	R×P	R-B8ch
37	K-R2	B-B5ch
38	B-N3	B×Bch
39	K×B	R-KB3
40	N-K5	R-B6ch
41	K-R2	N-B5

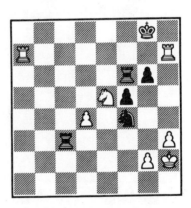

CHESS 4.6 now announces mate in four!

42	R(QR7)-KN7ch	K-B1
43	N-Q7ch	K-K1
44	R-N8ch	R-B1
45	R×R mate	

White: CHESS 4.6
Black: Zvonko Vranesic

London, September 1977
Sicilian Defence

1	P-K4	P-QB4
2	N-KB3	P-K3
3	P-Q4	P×P
4	N×P	N-KB3

5	N-QB3	B-N5
6	P-B3	

Best is 6 P-K5, which is known to lead to an advantage for White after a complicated sequence. CHESS 4.6 did not know this variation and was uanble to calculate the consequences of 6 P-K5 with sufficient accuracy. It therefore discovered a "new" move.

6	...	0-0
7	B-KB4	P-QR3
8	P-QR3	B-R4?!

8...B × Nch 9 P × B P-Q3 is more solid.

9	B-Q6	R-K1
10	P-QN4	B-B2
11	N-N3	B × B
12	Q × B	Q-K2

Necessary, in order to reduce White's grip on the dark squares.

13	Q × Q	R × Q
14	P-K5!	

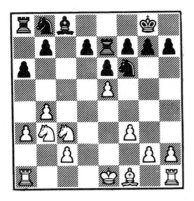

As this move demonstrates, Black's troubles on the dark squares are not yet over, because after

14	...	N-Q4

White can continue 15 N-K4 and

then N-Q6.

15	K-Q2?	

Lack of positional appreciation.

15	...	N × N
16	K × N	N-B3
17	R-K1	P-QN4
18	B-Q3	R-N1
19	K-N2	P-Q4?

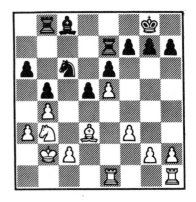

Black expects to be able to regain the pawn but as usual the program calculates better than its human opponent.

20	P × P e.p.	R-Q2
21	R-Q1	

The move that Vranesic had overlooked. If now 21...R × P?? 22 B × RPch K × B 23 R × R.

21	...	N-K4
22	N-B5	R-Q1
23	P-KB4	N-N5
24	P-Q7!	

The same motif. If 24...B × P 24 N × B R × N 26 B × RPch K × B 27 R × R.

24	...	B-N2
25	R-Q2	B-Q4
26	N × RP	R-N3
27	N-B5	N-B3
28	P-QR4!	

White temporarily returns one of his extra pawns in order to create three connected passed pawns on the Q-side.

28	...	P×P
29	P-B4!	B-R1

If 29...R×NPch 30 K-B3, winning a piece.

30	K-B3	P-N3
31	B-B2	P-R6
32	K-N3	B-B3
33	K×P	K-B1
34	B-R4	B×B
35	K×B	K-K2

36	R(1)-Q1	R-QR1ch
37	K-N3	R-Q1
38	P-N5	P-R3
39	K-N4	R(3)-N1
40	P-N3	R-QR1
41	P-N6	R(R)-N1
42	K-N5	P-N4
43	P×P	P×P
44	R-Q6	N-N5
45	N-R6	R-QR1
46	P-N7	R-R2
47	P-N8=Q	R×Qch
48	N×R	R-N2ch
49	R-N6	R×P
50	RxRch	K-B3

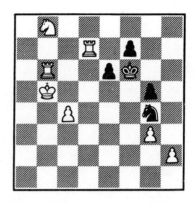

It is almost superfluous to comment on the strength of White's position but the sixty move rule (see page 88) offers Black some hope. He must try, at all costs, to avoid walking into a forced mate within the next ten moves.

51	P-B5	N-K4
52	P-B6	K-N3

From a practical point of view Black might have tried 52...N×P and hoped to avoid mate for long enough to win on time.

53	P-B7	N×R
54	N×N	K-B4
55	P-B8=Q	K-N3
56	Q-KN8ch	K-B4
57	Q-R7ch	K-N5
58	N-K5 mate	

"I am very impressed" - Vranesic.

White: CHESS 4.6
Black: Zvonko Vranesic

London, September 1977
Sicilian Defence

1	P-K4	P-QB4
2	N-KB3	P-K3
3	P-Q4	P×P

4	N × P	N-QB3
5	N × N	

CHESS 4.6 always seems to make this capture in the Sicilian Defence even though it is usually bad (of my own game against the program, page 10). Although Black's QRP is isolated, Black has an important pawn majority in the centre and the use of the QN-file.

5	...	NP × N
6	B-K3	N-B3
7	N-B3	P-Q4
8	P-K5	N-Q2
9	P-B4	B-K2
10	B-K2	0-0
11	0-0	P-QR4
12	B-Q3	P-KB4

12...P-QB4 seems more natural.

13	P × P e.p.	N × P
14	Q-B3	R-N1
15	B-Q4	P-B4
16	B-K5	P-B5?

The program did not overlook the capture of the rook, it misassessed the position that arises after Black's 18th move.

17	B × R	Q-N3ch
18	K-R1	Q × B

19	B-K2	Q × NP
20	KR-B1	Q-N3
21	QR-N1	Q-B2
22	Q-N3	B-B4
23	R-K1	B-Q2
24	R-KB1	B-Q3
25	N-N5	B × N
26	R × B	N-K5
27	Q-KR3	R-B3
28	B-N4	Q-Q2?

Overlooking a simple, tactical reply.

29	R × QP	Q-K2
30	R × P	P-R3
31	Q-K3	N-B4
32	B-K2	Q-QB2
33	R-R8ch	K-R2
34	P-N3	P-K4

A final, desparate blow directed against White's K-side.

35	P × P	R × Rch
36	B × R	B × P
37	P-QR4	B-B3
38	B-N2	N-Q2
39	R-R7	Q-Q3
40	Q-K4ch	P-N3
41	Q-Q5	

In this hopeless position Vranesic lost on time. Whether or not he exchanges queens Black will lose his knight.

4   Computer Chess Tournaments

Since 1970 the Association for Computing Machinery (ACM) has organized a chess tournament as part of its annual conference. In 1974 the first World Championship for computer programs took place in Stockholm. Since then computer tournaments have become increasingly popular, with events taking place in Germany, Canada, the Netherlands as well as the annual tournament in the U.S.A. In 1978, the first competition exclusively for microcomputers was held - a suggestion of my own which was implemented thanks to Douglas Penrod, founder/editor of the *Computer Chess Newsletter*. There is now an international society for those interested in computer chess and it looks as though interest in the subject is increasing at an almost exponential rate, which is perhaps not so surprising in view of the advent of home computing as a hobby.

The two principal computer chess tournaments continue to be the annual ACM competition and the World Championship which is held every three years. I have written books on the 1975 and 1976 ACM events; this chapter and Appendix B of this volume are devoted to coverage of the 1977 ACM tournament in Seattle and the Second World Comptuer Championship which was held in Toronto earlier in the same year.

Second World Computer Championship
Toronto, August 7th-9th 1977

No.	Program	Rd 1		Rd 2		Rd 3		Rd 4		Total	Place
1	CHESS 4.6 (USA)	W11	1	B 9	1	W2	1	B 4	1	4	1st
2	DUCHESS (USA)	W3	1	B 14	1	B 1	0	B 9	1	3	2nd =
3	KAISSA (USSR)	B 2	0	W16	1	B 5	1	B 6	1	3	2nd =
4	BELLE (USA)	W6	½	B 12	1	W7	1	W1	0	2 ½	4th =
5	CHAOS (USA	W15	1	B 7	½	W3	0	B 12	1	2 ½	4th =
6	BLACK KNIGHT (USA)	B 4	½	W8		B 14	1	W3	0	2	6th =
7	DARK HORSE (Sweden)	B 16	1	W5		B 4	0	B 10		2	6th =
8	ELSA (W. Germany)	W16		B 6		W9	0	B 15	1	2	6th =
9	MASTER (England)	B 13	1	W1	0	B 8	1	W2	0	2	6th =
10	WITA (Canada)	B 14	0	B 11	1	W15		W7		2	6th =
11	BCP (England)	B 1	0	W10	0	B 16	1	W14		1	11th =
12	BLITZ V (USA)	B 8		W4	0	B 13	1	W5	0	1	11th =
13	CHUTE 1.2 (Canada)	W9	0	B 7		W12	0	B 16	1	1	11th =
14	OSTRICH (Canada)	W10	1	W2	0	W6	0	B 11		1	11th
15	BS 6676 (Netherlands)	B 5	0	W13		B 10		W8	0	1	15th
16	TELL (Switzerland)	W7	0	B 3	0	W11	0	W13	0	0	16th

The sensation of the tournament was KAISSA's loss to DUCHESS in the first round. KAISSA, the defending World Champion, had been seeded number one, but played very much below the level that I had expected. Full credit must go to DUCHESS which demonstrated that it had made a greater improvement during the preceding year than any other program. The

DUCHESS-KAISSA game is annotated below but for reasons of space I have decided to depart from my usual pattern and am giving the remainder of the games from this event (and all of the games from ACM 77) in Appendix B, without notes.

White: DUCHESS

Black: KAISSA

Centre Counter

1	P-K4	P-Q4

KAISSA's favourite defence.

2	P × P	N-KB3
3	P-Q4	N × P
4	N-KB3	P-KN3
5	B-K2	B-N2
6	P-B4	N-N3
7	N-B3	0-0
8	B-K3	B-N5
9	P-B5	

This move drives Black's knight off ...QN3 so that White's eleventh move attacks the black QNP.

9	...	N-Q4
10	0-0	P-K3
11	Q-N3	P-N3

Now or on the previous move Black should have considered the exchange ...N × B.

12	N × N	P × N
13	B-KN5	Q-Q2
14	P-KR3	B-B4

15	Q-B3	R-K1
16	KR-K1	B-K5
17	N-Q2	Q-B4

Somewhat pointless. While White has been playing fairly methodically, improving its position very slightly move by move, KAISSA has been floundering around without any sort of plan in sight. Black should be aiming to complete its development.

18	B-K3	Q-K3
19	N × B	P × N

If 19...Q × N 20 B-KR6!, followed by B-QN5.

20	P × P	BP × P
21	KR-QB1!	

Keeping the QB-file firmly under control, White makes it clear that the Black knight will not find it easy to reach a comfortable square.

21	...	N-Q2
22	B-N4	Q-Q4
23	Q-B6	N-B3
24	B-K2	QR-Q1
25	Q-R4	R-K2
26	B-QN5	Q-KB4
27	R-B2	N-Q4

At last the knight has reached a sensible looking square but it is too late to do anything about the invasion of the QB-file by White's major pieces.

28	R(1)-QB1	B-B3
29	Q-N3	P-QR4
30	P-N4	Q-K3
31	R-B6	

The invasion of Black's position is complete. For KAISSA there is no satisfactory move.

31	...	P-R5
32	Q×P	R-Q3
33	R×R	Q×R
34	Q-R8ch	

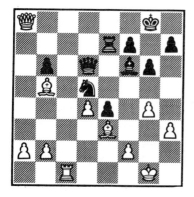

34	...	R-K1

I had expected KAISSA to play 34...K-N2, which allows White to win a piece by 35 P-N5. When KAISSA played its rook back to K1 I commented to the audience that I thought there must be a bug in the program. How else could one explain away the voluntary loss of the rook? Nobody, not even ex-World Champion Botvinnik, who was sitting in the audience, could suggest why KAISSA had played this move, and its programmers, Messrs Donskoy and Arlazarov, agreed that the answer was a bug.

Later that night however, the programmers reset this position in order to see what their program had been thinking about. The result was astounding: KAISSA had seen the continuation 34...K-N2 35 Q-KB8ch!! K×Q 36 B-KR6ch followed by R-B8ch and a forced mate.

The time is fast approaching when I am going to have to admit that chess programs are smarter than I am.

35	Q×Rch	K-N2
36	P-N5	

Now 36 Q-KB8ch does not work because after 36...K×Q 37 B-KR6ch the black king can escape to K2, which square was previously occupied by Black's rook.

36	...	B-Q1
37	B-QB4	Q-K2
38	Q×Q	N×Q
39	B-B4	N-B4
40	B-Q5	K-B1
41	R-B8	K-K2
42	R-B4	N-N2
43	B×KP	N-K3
44	B-K3	N-B2
45	P-Q5	N-N4
46	B-B3	K-Q2
47	P-QR4	N-Q3
48	R-B6	N-B4

and KAISSA's programmers resigned for their program.

After KAISSA's loss in this game, the hoped-for clash between KAISSA and CHESS 4.6 did not take place because of the way that the Swiss pairing system operates. The same situation occurred in the first World Computer Championship in Stockholm - CHESS 4.0 lost in an early round and was never paired against KAISA. The spectators (and the programmers) were naturally anxious to see what would happen when these two giants of the computer chess world met in mortal combat, so the same solution was applied to this situation as had been employed in Stockholm three years earlier. An exhibition game was arranged, after the tournament, between KAISSA and CHESS 4.6. Since CHESS 4.0 had White in their Stockholm encounter (which was drawn) I suggested that KAISSA be given White for the Toronto game, and no-one objected.

White: KAISSA
Black: CHESS 4.6

Toronto 1977
Nimzowitsch's Defence

1	P-K4	N-QB3

An unusual move (in human chess) which can lead to interesting positions after only a few moves.

2	N-KB3	P-K3
3	P-Q4	P-Q4
4	B-Q3	

4 N-B3 or 4 P-K5 would give White more chance of keeping the advantage.

4	...	P×P
5	B×P	B-Q2
6	0-0	N-B3
7	R-K1	N×B
8	R×N	B-K2
9	P-B4	

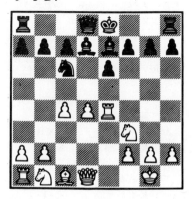

Black has equalized and should continue with 9...B-B3.

9	...	P-B4?

A weak move, leaving a backward pawn on K3 and a weak square on K4.

10	R-K1	0-0
11	N-B3	P-B5

Somewhat artificial but quite well motivated. Black's KBP restricts White's bishop and cramps his K-side.

12	Q-Q3	Q-K1
13	P-KN3?	

Opening up the KB-file which can be used by Black for an attack against the White king. This move also allows Black to exchange off a potentially weak pawn.

13	...	P×P
14	RP×P	Q-B2
15	B-B4	P-KN4!

Striking out in the right direction - towards White's king.

16 P-Q5

The best chance for counterplay.

16 ...   P × P?

A tactical miscalculation and a strategic error as well. Firstly CHESS 4.6 overlooks the effect of 17 (which KAISSA does not play) and secondly it is far more sensible to proceed with the K-side attack by 16...P × B rather than be diverted to another arena.

17 QN × P??

This leads to a position in which White has slightly the better ending. Instead, 17 R × B would have kept White very much in the game, e.g. 17...Q × R 18 N × QP or 17...N × R 18 N × NP.

17	...	P × B
18	N × Bch	N × N
19	Q × B	N-N3
20	Q × Qch	R × Q
21	P-KN4	R-Q2

The ending is marginally better for White because Black's K-side pawns are isolated, but in a game between two strong human opponents I would expect the result to be a draw. From now on however, CHESS 4.6 demonstrates that its slightly deeper exhaustive search is extremely useful in certain situations.

22	QR-Q1	QR-Q1
23	R × R	R × R
24	K-N2	K-N2
25	N-N5??	

Already a fatal error. The Black root must not be allowed onto the seventh rank.

25	...	R-Q7
26	R-QN1	R-B7

27	P-N3	N-K4
28	R-KR1	R × RP
29	R-R4	

After 29 R × Pch K-N3 30 R-K7 K × N 31 R × Nch K × P, Black is a pawn up with an easy endgame win.

29	...	N-Q6
30	N-R3	R-N7
31	P-N5	K-N1

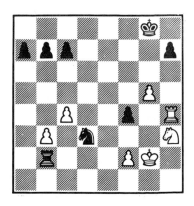

32 N × P??

Making Black's task simple. Up to this point I had grave doubts as to whether CHESS 4.6 would be able to force a win against a careful defense but it seems that KAISSA did not know about one of the golden rules of endgame play - when you are a pawn or two down you should exchange pawns but not pieces.

32	...	R × BPch
33	K-N3	R × N
34	R × R	N × R
35	K × N	K-B2
36	P-N4	K-K3
37	K-K4	P-QR3
38	K-B4	K-Q3
39	K-K4	P-B4

Creating a passed pawn.

40	P × Pch	K × P
41	K-Q3	P-R4
42	K-B3	P-R5

43	K-Q3	K-N5
44	K-B2	K × P

KAISSA's programmers resigned.

Eighth ACM Computer Championship
Seattle, October 15th-17th 1977

No.	Program	Rd 1		Rd 2		Rd 3		Rd 4		Total	Place
1	CHESS 4.6	W8	1	B 4	1	W3	1	B 2	½	3½	1st
2	DUCHESS	B 6	1	W5	1	B 7	1	W1	½	3½	1st =
3	CHAOS	W10	1	B 12	1	B 1	0	W6	1	3	3rd
4	XENARBOR	W11	1	W1	0	B 5	1	B 8	½	2½	4th
5	BLACK KNIGHT	W9	1	B 2	0	W4	0	B 11	1	2	5th =
6	BLITZ V	W2	0	B 8	1	W12	1	B 3	0	2	5th =
7	OSTRICH	B 12	0	W9	1	W2	0	B 10	1	2	5th =
8	CHUTE 1.2	B 1	0	W6	0	B 10	1	W4	½	1½	8th
9	BRUTE FORCE	B 5	0	B 7	0	W11	0	W12	1	1	9th =
10	TYRO	B 3	0	B 11	1	W8	0	W7	0	1	9th =
11	WITA	B 4	0	W10	0	B 9	1	W5	0	1	9th =
12	8080 CHESS	W7	1	W3	0	B 6	0	B 9	0	1	9th =

This tournament was notable for the appearance, for the first time in the history of the event, of a chess program running on a microprocessor (8080 Chess). Although the program did not perform well, and its sole point came about from good fortune rather than good play, its participation was a nudge in the ribs for the big programs running on much larger and faster machines. In future years I would hope that the leading programs in each year's microprocessor tournament will be allowed to compete with the 'big guys' in the ACM tournaments. Just as computer chess tournaments have done much to stimulate work in the field, so the competition between small and large machines will probably inspire microprocessor programmers to find new programming strategies that are not limited by small trees and slower machines.

Probably everyone expected that the eighth ACM. tournament would be won with a 100% score by CHESS 4.6, just as so many previous events had been won by this program's predecessors. Before the start, and right up to the middle of the last round, this was my opinion. In fact, I rather rashly gave odds of 100 to 1 that if the CHESS 4.6 v DUCHESS game ended in a decisive result then the Northwestern program would be the winner. My co-author risked a dollar, which he retrieved, and I had a few anxious moments in the endgame, when DUCHESS had the better position. For the games of this event the reader is referred to Appendix B.

During the tournament I gave a simultaneous exhibition against all twelve programs. In a similar match in 1975 I had scored ten wins and two draws. This time I again won ten, but drew one and lost one, to CHESS 4.6. The time has come when I can no longer hold off the world's strongest program when giving it only a fraction of my concentration. Ten years ago this possibility would have seemed extremely remote.

5 Microcomputers and Chess

Researchers who first described how computers might be programmed to play chess were talking about machines costing millions of dollars. These machines occupied entire laboratories, ran on vacuum tubes or mechanical relays, required large amounts of electricity, generated vast amounts of heat, and failed at intervals measured in minutes or hours. They executed approximately 10,000 instructions per second, compared with 10,000,000 or more on some big fast machines currently available. They had to be programmed in machine language, a language that must have driven a certain number of programmers in the 1950's into a permanent state of insanity. Memory space was measured in bits rather than in kilowords as it is now, thereby placing severe restrictions on the size of programs. Finding mistakes in programs was a tremendous task. Programmers complained that their programs failed because of hardware problems while the technicians called in to find the mysterious bugs countered that the problems were with the programs. The two were always seen working together and blaming each other for their own woes.

The first chess programs were developed in such an environment, and it is little wonder they didn't play particularly strong chess. The first program, in fact, played on a 6 x 6 board (without Bishops) because of limitations caused by these factors.

In the 1960's, transistors replaced vacuum tubes and relays and the second generation of computers was born. Computer centers sprang up at a large number of universities, research centers, and commercial establishments. They were supported by staffs of dozens of programmers, system analysts, operators and technicians. High level languages such as FORTRAN became available as did editors, assemblers, compilers, and operating systems. Time sharing systems became the rule - a single computer servicing as many as a hundred users with each being oblivious of the other's presence. Charges for computing time typically ran from $5 to $10 per minute.

Smaller computers called minicomputers also started to be produced by several firms. Rather than costing millions of dollars and requiring a large staff to maintain, these systems cost $50,000 - $200,000 and were kept running by small staffs of two or three. They found their way into the laboratories of universities, mainly in engineering and computer science departments, although as time went on and costs dropped, they invaded other departments as well including geography, music, and linguistics. They differed from their larger brothers mainly in (1) their word size: typically 12 to 24 bits (2) memory size: ranging from 4K to 64K words, (3) their ability to support a number of users; they could support only one person at a time, (4) the peripheral equipment they could control: usually much less and slower, and (5) the cost of using them: once acquired there was often no charge for computer time.

Throughout the 1960's and early 1970's great advances were made in computer hardware and software. The third generation computers born in the late 1960's were characterized by the introduction of integrated circuits. These circuits crammed the electronic equivalent of a radio onto a piece of semiconductor material smaller than a penny. Computer systems of all sizes and prices became available from a lower limit of about $5,000 to as much as $20,000,000 and more.

By the middle 1970's, approximately 200 chess programs had been developed. The performances of a number of them are well known, but there are many others which never acquired much of a reputation. Many special endgame and mating programs also were written. Perhaps 500 - 2000 people around the world had taken a shot at programming chess in one way or another. Thousands of others were probably interested in programming chess but were restrained by the unavailability of computing facilities.

Paralleling the interest to program computers to play chess, people have shown an equal interest and desire to play against them. People love to play games and computers are becoming increasingly popular opponents. They never get upset when they lose (perhaps this is a negative consideration - maybe people like to see their opponent fret and fume and squirm!), they never tire and are always ready to start another game when the last one ends, they can play at any desired speed, they can be insulted, ridiculed, and ultimately unplugged! They never rave to their colleagues about victories or seek excuses for defeats. One can discuss strategy in their presence (for now anyway, until the day arrives when they listen!), eat, make noise, and in general, show them none of the courtesies normally given a warmblooded opponent. They serve as tireless teachers, having infinite patience. They become friends and often are talked to as though they are human.

For many years, game playing programs with small computing requirements have flourished on university campuses. STARTRECK, probably the most popular of these, has been a grand success for a number of years. While students of the 1950's and 1960's found themselves in academic difficulties because of excesses in bridge and other human versus human games, more recently electronic games have caused similar problems. Chess programs have been available on a number of computers but they have been used sparingly because of their large computing requirements. MAC HACK, various versions of COKO, BELLE, OSTRICH, and CHESS 3.0 - 4.6 have been widely distributed and are used after hours (when computing costs are lower) by thousands of chess enthusiasts.

In 1975, as a result of great progress in the miniaturization of transistor circuitry leading to the introduction of large scale integrated (LSI) circuits the microcomputer became commercially available at the retail store level. Computer circuitry that once occupied rooms and cost millions of dollars could now be manufactured for only several dollars and placed on the head of a penny. A revolution was born. Cost fell to the point where it became feasible for someone to have his own computer. For $1000, the cost of a good stereo system, an individual could purchase a computer for his own home, a computer more powerful than any in existence 25 years earlier. In the 1950's and 1960's, it was in vogue for the middle and upper class to spend hundreds of dollars on stereo equipment in order to obtain distortion-free sound at frequencies only their pet cats could appreciate. Starting in the late 1970's, the home computer has assumed in some sense the same role. This movement has only begun, but its prospects for the future are awesome. One never finishes building a computer system. There is always something else to add. First, one can add more memory, then a good floppy disc, then a video display, then a magnetic tape unit, then a new and faster processing unit, and then again more memory and on and on. While there is really only one thing that can be done with a stereo system - i.e., play records - the possible applications for home computers fathom the imagination. Today, almost every home in North America has several hundred dollars worth of stereo equipment; in twenty years they will all have several thousand dollars in computing equipment.

The capabilities of current microcomputers differ from those of minicomputers in essentially the same ways as minicomputers differ from larger computers. The differences are related to the 8-bit word size around which the calculating and control units of almost all microcomputers are designed. This is in contrast to the 12 to 24-bit word sizes used by minicomputers and 32 to 64-bit word sizes used by larger computers. These calculating and control units, called microprocessors, are manufactured by such well known semiconductor giants as Texas Instruments, Motorola, RCA, and Intel. They typically cost in the order of $50. The 8-bit word size has two important effects. First, arithmetic on numbers exceeding ± 128 is awkward! It is necessary to store numbers larger than ± 128 in two memory locations with the least significant bits stored in one location and the most significant bits stored in another. The basic arithmetic operations consequently are more complicated and take longer than on larger machines. Second, most instructions require several memory locations (two or three) because the problem of addressing (or referring to) memory locations requires it. This also causes a loss in speed. In a big machine, it usually requires three instructions to add two positive numbers in locations X and Y and store the results in a third location Z:

Instruction 1: Transfer X to the adder A
Instruction 2: Add Y to A forming X + Y

Instruction 3: Store A at Z.

These three instructions occupy three (consecutive) memory locations say M_1, M_2, and M_3: X, Y and Z occupy three locations also. The addition requires a minimum of six machine cycles:

Cycle 1: Get instruction from M_1,

Cycle 2: Decode and perform instruction, i.e., transfer the number in X to the adder A,

Cycle 3: Get next instruction from M_2,

Cycle 4: Decode and perform instruction, i.e., add Y to A,

Cycle 5: Get next instruction from M_3

Cycle 6: Decode and perform instruction, i.e., store A at Z.

Additional cycles may be necessary in order to decode the instructions if locations X, Y, or Z must be "indirectly addressed", a term whose definition is beyond the scope of this presentation. Typically, seven, rather than six, cycles might be required.

For a microcomputer, instead of three instructions, six instructions are necessary assuming that positive numbers larger than 128 are to be added. The three numbers stored in X, Y, and Z in the previous example would have to be stored in six locations, X_2 X_1, Y_2, Y_1, and Z_2, Z_1. Then the program would:

Instruction 1: Transfer X_1 to the adder A

Instruction 2: Add Y_1 to A forming $X_1 + Y_1$ and possibly a carry C.

Instruction 3: Store A in Z_1.

Instruction 4: Transfer X_2 to the adder A

Instruction 5: Add Y_2 and C to A forming $X_2 + Y_2 + C$.

Instruction 6: Store A in Z_2

These six instructions would most likely occupy eighteen consecutive memory locations and the addition would require about 13 or 14 machine cycles. Thus even if the two machines just described were designed of circuits capable of operating at the same speed, the microcomputer would take more than twice the time of the larger machine to carry out the equivalent operation.

Memory sizes on microcomputers currently range from 2K 8-byte words to 16K 8-byte words. This is about 1/10 the size of minicomputer memories and about 1/100 the size of large computer memories. A limit of 64K arises because two memory locations can store a number from 0 to $2^{16} = 64K$. This small memory size places restrictions on program sizes. The better chess programs, CHESS 4.6, DUCHESS, BELLE, and so on require considerably more memory space than this. OSTRICH 79s*, a special

---

*Available through Computer Game Programs, 1700 Ohio Savings Plaza, 1801 East Ninth St., Cleveland, Ohio 44114.

version of OSTRICH which is commercially available, runs on 16K 16-bit words. SARGON, currently the best of the microcomputer programs however only uses 16K of 8-bit words. Most of the big programs have between 5,000 - 20,000 instructions but in addition they use additional memory space to store information gathered while searching the move tree. In the case of CHESS 4.7, this can be as much as a million words! Other programs use anywhere from about 10K to 200K and more. OSTRICH 79S has about 8K instructions and requires about 8K for storing information about the move tree.

Not only are main memories smaller, secondary memories are also smaller. Secondary memory refers to disc and tape storage. In microcomputers, they are at least an order of magnitude smaller than they are on minicomputers and they also function more slowly. Secondary memory is used during program development and thus developing programs for microcomputers is a slower procedure than on big computers.

Software for microcomputers is getting more sophisticated but presently is way behind that available on larger systems. The only high level programming language widely available for microcomputers is BASIC and this executes in an "interpretive mode". In an interpretive mode, each BASIC instruction is translated into machine language as it is executed, resulting in relatively slow program execution when compared to programs which are completely translated before execution begins. Programs written for larger machines in FORTRAN, PL1, or other high level programming languages are almost always translated before execution.

All of the aforementioned problems will disappear in the next few years. Sixteen-bit microcomputers are already on the market and it won't be long before the microcomputer of tomorrow looks like the minicomputer of today. Software will improve quickly with high level languages such as FORTRAN becoming widely available by 1980. Soon it will be no handicap whatsoever to develop a chess program on microcomputer. In another ten years, there will be microcomputers as powerful as any large computer on the market today! Chess-playing machines the size of cigar boxes will then make mincemeat of the best human players! Beware, David!

The Programs

There are two different types of microcomputer systems used for playing chess. First, there are microcomputers which are designed only to play chess. In my opinion, the most notable of these are CHESS CHALLENGER and BORIS. Two others, COMPU-CHESS and CHESSMATE are also available but they play more weakly. Prices are in the range of $150 to $300 and are falling. The second type are general purpose microcomputers for which home-brewed chess programs have been developed. These machines, of course, can handle the usual variety of non-chess programs as well. The most notable programs in this category are SARGON II and MIKE. There are at least twenty others in existence but they are considerably weaker. Several hundred others are at various stages of development.

CHESS CHALLENGER

CHESS CHALLENGER is manufactured by Fidelity Electronics, a Chicago based firm that advertises itself as the "world's largest manufacturer of self-contained, microprocessor based board games." In addition to CHESS CHALLENGER, they also produce CHECKER CHALLENGER and an electronic backgammon machine. When CHESS CHALLENGER first appeared on the market, it played disasterously. It both accepted and made illegal moves. However, more recent versions play quite respectably and are no longer subject to this criticism. The system is neatly packaged, runs on batteries or plugs into the wall, and weighs about five pounds. Two versions are marketed - CHESS CHALLENGER "3" and CHESS CHALLENGER "10". The "10" version is far superior and I give it credit for playing at about the 1300 USCF level when running in its "tournament mode", one of ten different modes in which it can play. Given a certain position, the computer's response is not always the same; if two or more moves look about as good as one another, the computer picks one randomly. Certain opening lines are programmed. A Fairchild F8 8-bit microprocessor is the brains of the machine. The program requires 4K of ROM (Read Only Memory - memory which can be read but not changed) and ½K of RAM (Random Access Memory - memory which can be read and changed). The program resides in the ROM and uses the RAM to store information found as the search progresses. The program is similar to CHESS 3.0. It carries out forward pruning at all levels in the tree.

CHESS CHALLENGER 10 took on OSTRICH several months ago at McGill and an interesting game ensued. Neither side made a serious tactical error. OSTRICH's positional play however made the difference. With each trade, OSTRICH's position improved slightly. By move 26, OSTRICH had the game wrapped up. OSTRICH earned a provisional Quebec Chess Federation rating of 1508 this summer based on tournament play. QCF ratings are very similar to USCF ratings.

White: OSTRICH
Black: CHESS CHALLENGER

Move times in seconds are denoted after each move. OSTRICH was set to play at a speed of 140 seconds per move; CHESS CHALLENGER 10

played in tournament mode.

1	P-K4(B)	P-QB4(32)
2	N-KB3(B)	P-Q3(30)
3	B-N5ch(B)	B-Q2(77)
4	N-B3(53)	N-KB3(181)
5	Q-K2(60)	N-B3(182)

6 0-0(110)   P-K4(657)

CHESS CHALLENGER 10 takes eleven minutes to find this move. Lights blinking on the console from time to time told us that it had not crashed. This move weakens the queen pawn and causes long term problems for CHESS CHALLENGER 10.

7	**P-Q3(14)**	**N-Q5(199)**
8	**B × Bch(70)**	**Q × B(75)**
9	**Q-Q1(141)**	**B-K2(153)**
10	**B-N5(106)**	**...**

CHESS CHALLENGER 10 has developed nicely to this point - certainly as well as a 1300 level player. With the exception of its weak queen pawn, all its pieces are on good squares. For the next few moves, however, aimless play takes over.

10	**...**	**P-QR4(640)**
11	**P-KR3(160)**	**R-KN1(547)**
12	**P-R3(146)**	**P-R3(176)**
13	**B × N(121)**	**P × B(152)**
14	**K-R1(148)**	**P-R5(275)**
15	**N-Q5(223)**	**B-Q1(261)**
16	**P-B3(231)**	**N-N6(167)**
17	**R-R2(125)**	**R-QB1(392)**
18	**N-Q2(180)**	**...**

OSTRICH forces CHESS CHALLENGER 10 to give up its well positioned knight.

18	**...**	**N × N(174)**
19	**Q × N(92)**	**R-N3(174)**
20	**P-Q4(141)**	**B/P × P(160)**
21	**P × P(151)**	**Q-N4(80)**
22	**R-Q1(342)**	**Q-B5(238)**
23	**QR-R1(321)**	**R-B3(333)**
24	**N-K3(373)**	**Q × P(273)**
25	**Q × Q(233)**	**P × Q(131)**
26	**R × P(112)**	**...**

While no outright mistakes have been made, CHESS CHALLENGER 10 finds itself with poorly placed pawns.

26	**...**	**P-N4(123)**
27	**QR-Q1(179)**	**B-K2(146)**
28	**N-B5!(277)**	**R-B7(190)**

A move that reflects the horizon problem. R-B7 pushes the loss of a pawn, either the queen's or the knight's, over the search horizon of CHESS CHALLENGER 10.

29	**R/4-Q2(151)**	**R × R(90)**
30	**R × R(98)**	**P-R4(107)**
31	**R-Q5**	**...**

OSTRICH is more interested in winning the knight's pawn than the queen's pawn. CHESS CHALLENGER 10 doesn't seem to have algorithms that encourage centralizing the king in the end game, a necessary maneuver here.

31	**...**	**R-N1(161)**
32	**R × P/5(100)**	**R-N3(126)**
33	**R-N8 + (191)**	**B-Q1**
34	**N × P + (146)**	**K-K2(47)**
35	**N-B5 + (128)**	**K-Q2(77)**
36	**R-N4(153)**	**B-B2(92)**
37	**R × P(243)**	**R-N1(110)**

38	P-QN3(328)	B-N3(125)	44	N-N7 + (115)	K-K2(73)
39	P-B4(134)	B-B2(215)	45	R-B4(431)	B-Q3(90)
40	P-N3(125)	R-N1(83)	46	N-B5 + (103)	K-K3(246)
41	P-QN4(86)	R-K1(84)	47	R-B6(66)	R-Q1(197)
42	P-N5(63)	R-QN1(93)	48	P-QR4(54)	P-R5(54)
43	R-Q4'+ (37)	K-K3(47)	49	P × P(42)	Resigns

BORIS

Named after Bobby Fischer's 1974 opponent in Reykjavik, BORIS is made by Chafitz Inc. of Rockville, Maryland. It has gone through a series of revisions. The current version reflects the influence of David Slate and Larry Atkin who have been discussing their ideas with Chafitz during the last year. Recently, Slate and Atkin have been hired as consultants by Chafitz. BORIS is based on an F8 microprocessor, the same one used by Fidelity in CHESS CHALLENGER 3 and 10. It requires $2\frac{1}{2}$K of ROM and $\frac{1}{4}$K of RAM, the smallest amount of memory used by any program that plays "respectable" chess. BORIS carries out an iterated full-width search going as deeply as time allows. Because of the small amount of RAM, BORIS is unable to store much information as the search progresses. Moves are generated as needed, a necessary procedure.

BORIS is not quite as strong as CHESS CHALLENGER 10. It is, however, superior in its ability to interact with the user. It is able to recommend moves for its opponent. This is done by storing the continuation figured out for its own last move and then displaying the second move on this sequence when asked. It can change places with its opponent at any time in the middle of a game. Comments such as "I expected that," "illegal move," and "congratulations," add a nice touch. New versions that may be on the market by the time this book appears will have the ability to speak moves. An electronic chess board is also anticipated, according to Dan Newmayer of Chafitz.

MIKE

Although it might be hard for Americans to comprehend, the microcomputer revolution which began in California has spread well beyond the North American continent - even as far as the western countries of Europe - to England for example! It was in London that Mike Johnson, a programmer with the British Post Office, programmed his own Motorola 6800 system to play chess. The 6800 is to the microcomputer world as was the model T Ford to the automobile world. Named after its author, MIKE is written in assembly language and requires 10K to execute. Although the Motorola 6800 is a relatively slow microprocessor (it takes 2 microseconds to add together two 8-bit numbers), MIKE searches trees at a rate of about 200 nodes/sec, a most impressive statistic. This, of course, means that about 36,000 nodes are examined during the course of a three minute move.

In September 1978, MIKE won the first European Microcomputer Chess Championship. Participants included BORIS (2nd place) and CHESS CHALLENGER 10 (3rd place). The five round round-robin actually ended in a tie between MIKE and BORIS but MIKE defeated BORIS in a playoff for the $200 first place prize. Three months later, Johnson came to Washington, D.C. and guided MIKE through a most respectable performance in the ACM's Ninth North American Computer Chess Championship finishing with 1 1/2 points out of a possible 4. MIKE drew with SARGON II, BLACK KNIGHT, and BS6676. Its game with SARGON II is presented on pages 84-85.

SARGON II

SARGON II, the current king of the microcomputer chess world was named after an ancient Mesopotamian king of the same name. Its authors, the husband and wife team of Kathe and Dan Spracklan, have invested all their free time since September 1977 developing first, SARGON I, and then its successor SARGON II. Being both programmers and chess players, the Spracklans have been captured by the excitement of watching their protege progress. SARGON II is playing stronger chess than any of its microcomputer contemporaries; a rating of about the 1450-1500 USCF level seems to be the consensus of opinion. SARGON II runs on Z-80 based microcomputers such as the TRS-80 (Radio Shack's computer) and the fast Wavemate Jupitor III which uses a 4.3 megahertz clock. The program occupies $12\frac{1}{2}$K bytes and is growing. It carries out a full-width search at a rate of about 50 nodes/sec. When participating in the ACM's Washington tournament, SARGON carried out three level searches in about two minutes. Checking moves at the last ply caused search to be extended. The program has an exchange evaluator which carried out a careful analysis of exchanges at terminal nodes. The program's strength, to a good measure, can be credited to the performance of this algorithm. A book having about 4000 positions is also included in the program.

SARGON I captured first place at the West Coast Computer Faire's Microcomputer Chess Tournament in March of 1978. In so doing, it polished off five opponents without a loss. Deciding to take on the giants with an improved version called SARGON II, the Spracklans brought their Jupiter Wavemate III to Washington to participate in the ACM's annual tournament. Originally seeded eighth in a field of twelve, SARGON II mildly surprise the competition by finishing with 2 1/2 out of 4 points. This placed it in a three-way tie for third place with CHAOS and BLITZ 6.5. The program's most impressive game was a victory over Tony Marsland's much improved AWIT in the final round. We present here its draw with MIKE one round earlier. In this game, SARGON II shows strength in gaining a two pawn advantage and then weakness in failing to understand how to proceed.

White: MIKE

Black: SARGON II

1	P-K4	P-K4
2	P-Q4	N-QB3
3	P-Q5	N-N5
4	P-QB3	N-R3
5	P-KB4	N-B4
6	P × P	...

Stronger is B-Q3. This prevents 6 ... Q-R5 + while simultaneously developing a bishop. MIKE would much rather bag a pawn.

6	...	Q-R5ch
7	K-Q2	N × Pch
8	K-B2	N-B7
9	Q-K1	...

Again, MIKE is better off with the developing move 9 N-B3.

9	...	B-B4
10	N-B3	Q-R4
11	R-N1	N-K2
12	B-K3	Q-N3 +
13	K-B1	B × B
14	Q × B	N-N5
15	Q-Q2	P-Q3
16	B-Q3	Q-R4
17	B-N5ch	B-Q2
18	B × Bch	K × B
19	P × P	P × P
20	P-KR3	N-KB3
21	Q-N5	Q × Q
22	N × Q	KR-KB1
23	P-B4	QR-B1
24	N-Q2	N/7 × P

MIKE now is paying for his slow development. It will fall behind by two pawns by move 27.

25	K-N1	N-K6
26	N/5-K4	N × N
27	N × N	R × P
28	N-B3	P-B4
29	P-QR4	P-Q4
30	P-KN3	R-KB3
31	R-K1	P-Q5
32	N-N5	P-QR3
33	N × P	P-B5
34	P × P	R × N
35	R × N	R/3 × P
36	P-R5	R-Q8ch
37	K-R2	R-QR5ch
38	R-QR3	R/5 × Rch
39	P × R	R-Q7ch
40	K-N3	R-Q6ch
41	K-B4	R × KRP
42	R-Q1ch	K-B3
43	P-R4	...

SARGON II can win easily by advancing the two passed kingside pawns. However, the program gives a lot of credit to attacking moves and not enough relatively to advancing pawns in such a situation. Consequently SARGON II leaves the passed pawns on their original squares while fruitlessly attacking with the rook. SARGON II, only programmed to detect draws by repetition of position when an identical position is repeated on alternative moves, fails to avoid a slightly more complicated drawning sequence, and thus the game ends in a draw in seven more moves. Newer versions of the Spracklen program will handle this position correctly.

43	...	R-R4
44	K-N4	R-R5ch
45	K-N3	R-R6ch
46	K-B4	R-R4
47	K-N4	R-R5ch
48	K-N3	R-R6ch
49	K-B4	R-R4
50	K-N4	R-R5ch
		D r a w n b y repetition.

How to keep up with events

Two magazines have taken the lead in publishing articles on computer chess and chess on microcomputers. *Personal Computing,* 1050 Commonwealth Avenue, Boston, Mass. 02215, USA, provides the most extensive coverage, about ten pages of news items and invited articles every month. Editor Harry Shershow has expanded coverage with every successive issue. Material is divided between large and small computers. *Byte Magazine,* the most widely distributed magazine dedicated to microcomputers, has published a number of invited articles on computer chess. Their address is BYTE Publications Inc., 70 Main Street, Peterborough, New Hampshire 03458, USA.

6 Computer Chess Miscellany

Programs to solve chess problems

A number of people are interested in problems of the "White to play and mate in two" variety. Although these problems are not really part of chess (since the positions are normally quite artificial) the same techniques that are used in chess programming could easily be employed to solve problems. In fact the Northwestern program has, for some time, announced mate whenever it detected a forced mate within its horizon. A program could be made to find all mates within a certain number of moves simply by performing an exhaustive search to the required depth, and for this reason such a program would be, in my opinion, of little value. (But that is because I dislike both chess problems and exhaustive searches). Some of the microprocessor machines described above already solve such problems.

Programs to do Swiss system pairings

Various programs exist to perform the pairings for Swiss system tournaments. One such program was used at the 1976 Chess Olympiad in Haifa, Israel. It not only paired the teams for each round in accordance with the rules of the Swiss system, it also gave printouts, day by day, on which all the players could see at a glance the scores of every individual in the event.

At a tournament where the rounds are played at the rate of one per day (or even more slowly), such a program presents few problems. If there is a hardware fault or a communication problem the pairings can always be done by hand as a last resort. There is, however, a danger that if such a program were to be used for a large individual tournament of the type that is extremely common in the U.S.A. (many competitors and two or three rounds per day), it might lead to a state of utter chaos. Imagine the situation between rounds, when eight of the nine games have been played in an event and there is a break of only an hour or so before the next round is due to begin. Suddenly the computer goes down, or there is a line fault, or the terminal malfunctions. What does the tournament director do? He must pair the players by hand, so he needs a set of pairing cards on which are written the pairings and results for each player for all the previous rounds. This means that each time the program outputs the pairings for a round it should also print out an updated pairing card for use by the tournament director in cases of emergency. So far I have not heard of a program which will do this, even though it is (in my opinion) an essential failsafe device. I would hate to be a T.D. in a tournament with 500 angry players, eagerly waiting for their pairings, when something went wrong with the program and there was no backup system.

Openings Innovations

Chess is a game in which the frontiers of knowledge are continually being expanded. In every tournament and match played at the master level, some new idea or ideas are seen in the openings. There is no real reason why chess programs should not be able to discover openings innovations in certain types of position since innovations are often surprising moves and computer programs are prone to make surprising moves rather often.

Some months ago I happened to be analyzing a variation of the French Defence which leads to extremely sharp play - the kind that programs revel in. Eventually I noticed that in a certain position, reached in a master game in 1935, White had a crushing continuation which was overlooked both by the players of the time and by the openings monograph which was devoted entirely to this particular system of the French. O.K., so an International Master finds a new move in the openings; hardly a matter for the headlines. But I felt at the time that the position was so sharp that a good computer program might well find the same continuation. So at the 1977 ACM tournament in Seattle I asked Larry Atkin to try this position on the Northwestern program.

The game Chistiakov-Orlov, Moscow Championship 1935 opened:

1	P-K4	P-K3
2	P-Q4	P-Q4
3	N-QB3	B-N5
4	P-QR3	B × Nch
5	P × B	P × P
6	Q-N4	N-KB3
7	Q × NP	R-N1
8	Q-R6	P-N3
9	B-KN5	R-N3
10	Q-R4	QN-Q2
11	B-N5	P-B3

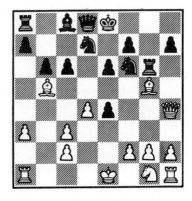

In this position Chistiakov retreated his bishop with 12 B-QB4. As pointed out in the book *"French Poisoned Pawn"* by Zeuthen and Jarlnaes (Copenhagen 1971), if White captures on QB6 with 12 BxP, Black plays 12...Q-B2 with an excellent game (13 BxR QxBPch and 14...QxR).

The innovation in the diagrammed position is 12 BxN! When the position was 'shown' to CHESS 4.6 it found the move 12 BxN in about 90 seconds, thereby improving on existing theory. After the program had printed out this move one of the spectators asked why Black cannot play 12...Q-B2 in reply - after all, White then has two bishops attacked and so must lose one of them. I asked Larry Atkin to make the reply move 12...Q-B2 but he informed me that it was not necessary. The program had predicted 12...Q-B2 as its main variation and had intended to continue 13 B-Q8!! This is probably what Chistiakov had missed. If Black does not capture the bishop on Q1 he is mated on K2 and if he plays 13...QxB then 14 QxQch KxQ 15 BxP R-N1 16 BxP leaves White two pawns up. The alternative to 12...Q-B2 is 12...RxB, but then comes 13 BxP Q-B2 14 P-Q5! (the difference - if White is allowed to capture on KB6 his queen will protect the QB3 pawn), when White will win.

After discovering this innovation CHESS 4.6 wrote a letter to the Readers' Questions column of the openings magazine *Modern Chess Theory,* and was told by Grandmaster Michael Stean that its new move was indeed correct!

Endgames

I described in my earlier volume *Chess and Computers* how I lost a case of whiskey to Dr. Arlazarov when he wrote a routine that would play perfectly in the ending of rook and pawn v rook. Since then a database has been created by Ken Thompson for the ending of queen v rook. This ending is a win, with correct play, for the side with the queen, but it is by no means an easy task for even a strong player to force the win within fifty moves*. Indeed, I well remember a good friend of mine defending just this ending in a World Student Team Championship, only to lose after forty-five of the fifty moves. Ken Thompson's program will always win this ending from the superior side and will always make the optimal defensive move when playing with the rook. Against masters, at speed chess, it rarely loses within fifty moves!

Professor Donald Michie has been developing a technique which he calls advice tables, whereby it is possible to program a computer to play such endgames by giving a set of heuristic rules (i.e. pieces of advice). This does not quite result in optimal play but it does result in sensible play without the

---

*A game is drawn if fifty successive moves are played by each side without a pawn being moved or a capture being made

need for exhaustive search. I wholeheartedly support any attempt to get away from brute force programming in chess and I therefore congratulate Michie for his invention of this technique.

Botvinnik's program PIONEER has been working on endgame studies with some success. I published an article by his colleague Stilman in my book on the 1976 U.S. Computer Chess Championship. When Botvinnik came to Toronto in 1977, he brought with him the Tree created by PIONEER to solve the following problem:

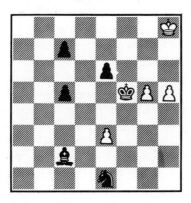

The Tree contains only 200 moves and was generated in 3½ hours of computing time.

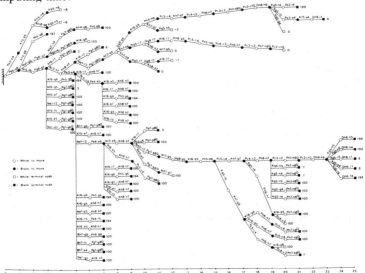

Fig. 13. Tree created by PIONEER to solve endgame problem in Fig. 12.

Reprinted courtesy of Academic Press, Advances in Computers, Vol. 18

Appendix A: An Unsolved Problem

It is a well-known empirical law of tree searching that the deeper the search the better the result. As chess programs, for example, search larger and larger trees, their performance improves. Many researchers in this field assume this law to guarantee ultimate success in chess programming, and in other problem domains that depend on heuristic search. I am not quite so convinced that this is the case. In my own opinion it is quite possible that deeper searches of the game tree will result in performances that asymptotically approach some fixed level and there is nothing to prove whether or not this level, in chess, will be at World Championship class.

I have long felt that there ought to be some theoretical method or computational experiment which would determine exactly how the parameters of the tree search affect the performance of the search. If a functional relationship could be found that related the performance of the tree searching system (P_t) to the branching factor (b), the depth of search (d) and the performance of the evaluation function (P_e), it would be possible to determine what increase in depth would be required in order to reach some desired performance level (e.g. World Chess Champion). In this chapter I shall describe an experiment which I think will solve this important problem and I leave it to others to implement my suggestion or to discover a theoretical alternative.

First let us define our problem domain and parameters. We shall assume that in our trees all paths are of depth d and that there are b branches at each non-terminal node. The evaluation function used to score the terminal nodes has performance P_e and the whole tree searching system has performance P_t.

P_e can be defined in various ways. It might be the correlation between the actual order of merit of a group of successor nodes (or moves) and the order of merit as determined by the evaluation function. Another possibility, and the one which I suggest is used for this experiment, is given by the expression

$$P_e = \frac{b + 1 - 2i}{b - 1} \qquad (1)$$

where i is the mean ranking of the move chosen by P_e in the actual order of merit. Note that if i = 1 (for which the evaluation function always chooses the best move),

$$P_e = \frac{1. \text{ If } i = (b + 1)}{(b + 1)/2}$$

(for which the evaluation function chooses at random), $P_e = 0$. If i = b (for which the worst move is always chosen), $P_e = -1$.

Similarly, P_t is given by

$$P_t = \frac{b + 1 - 2j}{b - 1} \qquad (2)$$

where j is the mean ranking of the move chosen at the root of the tree in the actual order of merit.

Clearly, when i = 1 and $P_e = 1$, j = 1 and $P_t = 1.-3 = 1$.

Next we must build a model of an evaluation function that conforms to (1). We shall assume that the b terminal node successors of the same parent node have scores S_1, S_2, S_3, ... S_b, which are generated randomly on the range $0 \leqslant S_k \leqslant R$. If we add, to each of these scores S_k, a different random number S^1_k generated on the range $-E \leqslant S^1_k \leqslant E$, then we have two sets of scores for the same group of nodes: S_1, S_2, ..., S_b and $S_1 + S^1$, $S_2 + S^1_2$, $S_3 + S^1_3$ ..., $S_b + S^1_b$.

If we look for the best score in the second group (let us assume that it is $S_3 + S^1_3$) we have, from the subscript 3, the fact that on this particular occasion our evaluation function (normally an inexact model) has picked the third best move as being best. By conducting a large number of experiments of this kind for various values of E it is possible to determine the mean value of i for each value of E. It is then possible to find a relationship between E and i so that we can produce a model of an evaluation function with any desired, positive value of P_e, simply by varying E.

(Note, incidentally, that $P_e = 1$ when E = 0 and $P_e = 0$ when E = ∞).

We are now ready to conduct the most important part of the experiment. For each group of b terminal nodes (all sharing a common parent node) generate the random scores S_1, S_2, S_3, ... S_b. Using some value of E (i.e. some value of P_e) generate the modified scores $S_1 + S_1$, ... etc., which are assigned to a similar group of nodes on a second tree. Perform a normal search of both trees, generating terminal scores in the manner described above. We will then have determined which move, at the root of the tree, would be chosen by the search of the tree with modified terminal scores. By determining where, in the actual order of merit (as found by the search of the unknown tree), this chosen move lies, we have the index j from which we can calculate P_t using (2).

By conducting a large number of experiments for different values of b, d and E, we will be able to derive a relationship expressing P_t as a function of P_e, b and d.

Applications

The most interesting application of this relationship is that it will enable us to estimate the depth of search necessary before (say) CHESS 4.6 can beat Bobby Fischer. I conjecture that for a World Champion, P_t lies somewhere around 0.99 (I estimate j to be around 1.15).

Another useful experiment would be to determine the effect of forward pruning. One could determine the relationship between P_t, P_e, b and d when a certain fraction f of the nodes at each non-terminal level were pruned, using an evaluation function of performance P_{pr} to do the pruning.

Further studies

The experiments described above can first be performed with trees for which the terminal scores are randomly generated. In a game situation however, there is some relation between the scores of the nodes in any successor group - this relationship being the fact that these successor nodes share the same parent. The significance of this fact can be seen from the following tree.

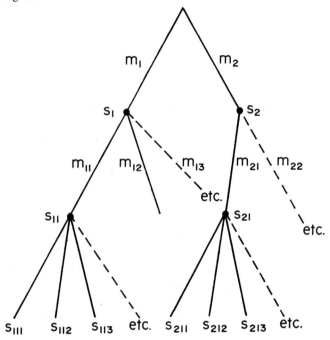

Let us assume that m_1 is a bad move which loses the queen to the reply m_{11} but that m_2 is a respectable move which does not lose material to the best reply m_{21}. Then the scores s_{111}, s_{112}, s_{113}, ... etc., and s_{211}, s_{212}, si_{213}, ... etc., are not random scores but are separated by the fact that in one group the scores will, in general, be much higher than those in the other group because of the enormous difference caused by the loss of the queen. Clearly even though the evaluation function may not choose the best move in either or both of the two groups, the tree search is still likely to prefer m_2 to m_1.

In order to allow for this effect the experiments should be performed on trees that have been grown to simulate game situations. Typically, in chess, there is a small number of moves (normally less than four) which appear either to maintain the status quo or to improve one's position. There is a larger number of moves which are slightly disadvantageous and more moves which are extremely disadvantageous. A graph of the apparent change in score brought about by making the nth best move in a chess position will look something like this.

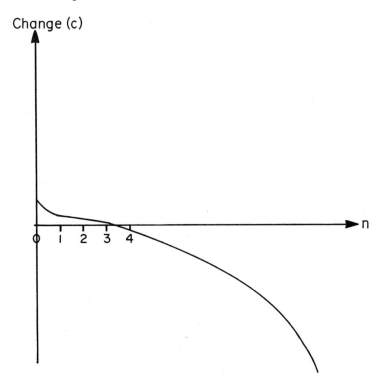

If we choose some function $f(n) = c_n$ which approximates to this curve we can determine the score for the nth best successor of a node (whose own score is s) from the equation

$$s_n = s + f(n + E_n)$$

where E_n is some number randomly generated on the range $-\frac{1}{2} \leqslant E_n \leqslant \frac{1}{2}$.

Now, starting at the root of the tree, we can grow the tree and assign apparent scores for all the nodes down to terminal depth in such a way as to simulate a chess tree. Then the tree can be searched in the manner described above.

If these experiments lead to the conclusion that exhaustive search techniques are not going to produce a World Chess Champion then those programmers who have placed all their faith in the search of enormous trees will try a different approach, possibly with greater success. I shall be very pleased to hear from any reader who performs these experiments and/or discovers a theoretical solution to the problem.

Appendix B: Games from 1977 Tournaments
Eighth ACM Tournaments
Round 1

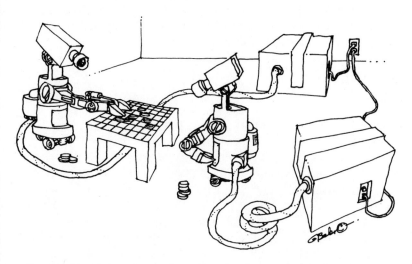

Reprinted, with permission, from Creative Computing, *Vol. 2, No. 1*

White: CHAOS
Black: TYRO

Queen's Gambit Declined

1 P-Q4 P-Q4 2 P-QB4 P-K3 3 N-QB3 N-KB3 4 B-N5 P-KR3 5 B×N P×B 6
P×P P×P 7 N-B3 B-QN5 8 P-KN3 0-0 9 B-N2 B×Nch 10 P×B R-K1 11
Q-Q2 K-N2 12 0-0 B-B4 13 Q-N2 P-N3 14 N-R4 Q-Q2 15 N×Bch Q×N 16
P-QB4 P-B3 17 P×P P×P 18 Q-N5 R-Q1 19 P-K4 Q-Q2 20 Q×QP N-B3
21 Q×Q R×Q 22 P-K5 R-QB1 23 B-R3 R(B1)-B2 24 P×Pch K×P 25
B×R R×B 26 QR-B1 N×P 27 K-N2 N-K7 28 KR-Q1 N×R 29 R×R
N×P 30 R×RP N-N5 31 K-B3 N-Q4 32 K-K2 P-N4 33 K-Q3 N-K2 34 R-N7
N-N3 35 R×NP N-K4ch 36 K-K4 N-N5 37 P-B3 N×P 38 R-N1 K-K3 39 R-
KR1 P-B4ch 40 K-B4 N×P 41 RPch K-B2 42 K×N K-N2 43 R-QN6 K-B2
44 K-B4 K-K2 45 K×P K-Q2 46 K-B6 K-B2 47 R-K6 K-Q2 48 P-N4 K-B2
49 P-N5 K-Q2 50 P-N6 K-B2 51 P-N7 K-Q2 52 P-N8=Q K-B2 53 Q-B7ch
K-Q1 R-K8mate.

White: BLACK KNIGHT
Black: BRUTE FORCE

Centre Counter

1 P-K4 P-Q4 2 P×P Q×P Q×P 3 N-QB3 Q-K3ch 4 KN-K2 B-Q2 5 P-Q4

N-QR3 6 B-N5 P-R3 7 B-K3 Q-QN3 8 Q-N1 P-N4 9 P-KR4 P×P 10 P-Q5
Q-N5 11 B-Q4 P-K4 12 P×Pe.p P-KB3 13 P-R3 Q-K2 14 P×Bch K-Q1 15
Q-R2 P-QB4 16 0-0-0 P×B 17 N×P N-B4 18 B-B4 Q-N2 19 N-K4 Q×NP
20 N×N Q-N4ch 21 R-Q2 Q×Rch 22 K×Q B×N 23 N-K6ch K×P 24
N×Bch K-B2 25 B-Q5 N-K2 26 B×P QR-Q1ch 27 K-B3 R-QN1 28 Q-K6
N-N1 29 Q-B6ch K-Q1 30 Q-Q7mate.

White: XENARBOR
Black: WITA
King's Indian Defence
1 P-Q4 N-KB3 2 P-QB4 P-KN3 3 N-QB3 B-N2 4 P-K4 P-K3 5 N-KB3 P-Q3
6 P-KN3 N-QB3 7 B-N2 P-KR3 8 0-0 0-0 9 P-Q5 P×P 10 BP×P N-N1 11 B-
K3 R-K1 12 Q-B2 Q-K2 13 KR-Q1 N×KP 14 N×N Q×N 15 Q×P B×P
16 QR-N1 N-R3 17 Q×QP B-N2 18 N-Q4 B-K4 19 B×Q B×Q 20 B-N2 B-
B1 21 KR-QB1 B-QB4 22 P-QR4 P-B3 23 P-R5 R-N1 24 R×B N×R 25 N-
B6 B-B4 26 R-N5 P-R3 37 R-N6 P×N 28 P×P R×R 29 P×R R-K4 30 P-
B7 P-KR4 31 P-R4 P-R4 32 B-KB1 P-R5 33 B-Q4 P-R6 34 B×R P×B 35 B-
B4ch K-B1 36 K-R2 K-K2 37 P-B3 B-B1 38 P-B4 P×P 39 P×P N-Q2 40 B-
N3 B-N2 41 B-R2 K-B3 42 B-N3 K-N2 43 P-B5 P×P 44 B-Q5 B-B1 45 P-N7
P-R7 46 P×B = Q-B3 47 B×P P-B5 48 Q-B5 P-B6 49 Q-KN5ch Resigns.

White: 8080 CHESS
Black: OSTRICH
Centre Game
1 P-K4 P-K4 2 P-Q4 N-KB3 3 P×P N×P 4 N-KB3 B-B4 5 N-Q4 N-QB3 6
N×N B×Pch 7 K-K2 QP×N 8 Q×Qch K×Q 9 B-B4 B-Q5 10 P-B3 B-
N5ch 11 K-Q3 N-B7ch 12 K×B N×R 13 B-B4 B-K3 14 B-Q3 K-B1 15 N-
Q2 R-Q1ch 16 K-K3 N-B7 17 B×P N-N5ch 18 K-K2 R-R1 19 B-K4 N×RP
20 P-QN4 R-R5 21 P-N3 R-R4 22 P-R4 B-Q4 23 B-Q3 N-N5 24 P-B4 B-N7
25 R-KN1 B-R6 26 N-B3 P-R4 27 P×P R×P 28 N-Q4 N×P 29 B×N
KR×Bch 30 K-B3 P-QB4 31 N-K2 R×P 32 N-B4 B-K3 33 R-QB1 P-KN4
34 N-K2 R-R7 35 R-B3 B-B4 36 N-B1 R-Q7 37 B-K2 R-K5 38 B-Q3 Black
lost on time. Black's next move, 38... P-N5 mate, could not be printed
because of a program bug. The analysis part of the program was aware of
the mate, but crashed in the process of trying to print the move. Contest
rules forbid any program changes, so time ran out for Monty Newborn, the
author of Ostrich. The irony of the situation is that Monty was co-author of
this very rule!

White: CHESS 4.6
Black: CHUTE

Ruy Lopez

1 P-K4 P-K4 2 N-NB3 N-QB3 3 B-N5 KN-K2 4 P-Q4 P×P 5 N×P N×N 6 Q×N 6 Q×N P-QR3 7 B-K2 N-B3 8 Q-B4 B-Q3 9 B-K3 0-0 10 N-B3 P-QN4 11 Q-Q5 B-N2 12 0-0 Q-K1 13 P-QR3 Q-K3 14 P-B4 QR-K1 15 Q×Q BP×Q 16 QR-Q1 P-K4 17 P-B5 N-K2 18 P-QN3 R-B3 19 P-QN4 R-R1 20 B-N5 R-B2 21 B-R5 P-N3 22 B×B B×B 23 P×P R×Rch 24 K×R R-KB1ch 25 K-K1 B-R5ch 26 P-N3 B×NPch 27 P×B P×P 28 B×P R-B6 29 R-Q3 R×R 30 P×R K-N2 31 B-B5 P-Q3 32 N-Q5 P-B3 33 N-N6 K-R1 34 N-B8 P-Q4 35 N-Q6 B-R1 36 P×P P×P 37 B-B8 P-K5 38 B×P B-B3 39 B×P B×B 40 N×B P×P 41 P-R4 K-N2 42 P-R5 K-R3 43 P-R6 K-R4 44 P-R7 P-Q7ch 45 K×P K-N5 46 P-R8=Q K×P 47 N-R3 P-Q5 48 P-N5 K-B7 49 P-N6 K-N6 50 Q-K4 K-B7 51 P-K7 K-N8 52 P-N8=Q K-B7 53 Q-K1ch K-N7 54 Q(N8)-KN3mate.

White: BLITZ
Black: DUCHESS

Ruy Lopez

1 P-K4 P-K4 2 N-KB3 N-QB3 3 B-N5 P-QR3 4 B×N QP×B 5 P-Q4 P×P 6 Q×P Q×Q 7 N×Q B-Q2 8 B-K3 0-0-0 9 N-QB3 B-Q3 10 0-0-0 N-B3 11 R-Q3 N-N5 12 P-KN3 N×B R×N B-QB4 14 R-Q3 B-KN5 15 P-B3 B-R4 16 N(B3)-K2 B×N 17 N×B P-QB4 18 N-NB5 R×R 19 P×R B×P 20 R-B1 B-K7 21 N-K7ch K-Q1 22 R×P B×P 23 N-Q5 B×P 24 N×P R-N1 25 N-K6ch K-K1 26 R×KNP R×R 27 N×Rch K-K2 28 N-R5 K-Q3 29 N-B4 P-B5 30 K-Q2 B-N8 31 P-QR3 P-N4 32 P-KN4 K-K4 33 N-K2 B-Q6 34 P-KR4 B×N 35 K×B K-B5 36 P-N5 K-N5 37 K-B3 K×P 38 K-B4 P-QR4 39 K-B5 P-N5 40 P×P P×P 41 P-N6 P×Pch 42 K-K4 P-N4 43 K-Q4 P-N5 44 K×P P-KN6 45 K×P K-N4 46 K-R5 P-N7 47 P-N4 P-N8=Q 48 P-N5 Q-R2ch 49 K-N4 K-B4 50 K-B4 K-K4 51 K-N4 Adjudicated a win for Black.

Round 2

White: 8080 CHESS
Black: CHAOS

Sicilian Defence

1 P-K4 P-QB4 2 P-Q4 P×P 3 Q×P N-QB3 4 Q-Q5 N-B3 5 Q-Q3 P-K4 6 N-KB3 B-B4 7 B-N5 Q-N3 8 B×N B×Pch 9 K-Q2 Q×P 10 B×NP R-KN1 11 Q-B3 Q×Qch 12 K×Q R×B 13 N-Q2 P-Q3 14 N-B4 B-QB4 15 P-KR4 B-K3 16 N-N2 R-N5 White lost on time.

White: WITA
Black: TYRO

Queen's Gambit Declined

1 P-Q4 P-Q4 2 P-QB4 P-K3 3 P-K4 P × KP 4 N-QB3 B-N5 5 P-QR3 B × Nch 6 P × B N-KB3 7 R-N1 0-0 8 B-K2 P-QN3 9 B-B4 P-B3 10 N-R3 Q-K2 11 Q-R4 KN-Q2 12 0-0 B-R3 13 B × N N × B 14 KR-Q1 P-KB4 15 K-R1 P-K4 16 P × P Q × KP 17 Q-N3 K-R1 18 N-N5 Q-B3 19 N-R3 R-Q1 20 R × Rch Q × R 21 N-B4 Q-R5 22 P-N3 Q-B3 23 R-Q1 B-B1 24 N-R5 Q-K2 25 P-R3 P-N3 26 P-B5 P × N 37 P × P P × P 28 P-KB4 P-N4 29 B × RP B-K3 30 Q-N4 Q × Q 31 BP × Q B-Q4 32 P-N4 P × P 33 K-R2 P × P 34 P-B5 R × P 35 B-N4 R-R7ch 36 K × P N-Q2 37 B-R5 N-B3 38 K-R4 R-R7ch 39 K-N5 N × B 40 P-B6 K-N1 41 R-KN1 K-B2 42 R-QR1 N × P 43 K-B5 R-KB7ch 44 K-N5 P-R4 45 K-R6 R-KN7 46 R-R7ch K-K3 47 R-R1 P-K6 48 R-R6 K-B4 49 R-R2 R-N3mate.

White: CHUTE
Black: BLITZ

Petroff Defence

1 P-K4 P-K4 2 N-KB3 N-KB3 3 N × P P-Q3 4 N-KB3 N × P 5 Q-K2 Q-K2 6 P-Q3 N-KB3 7 B-N5 QN-Q2 8 Q × Qch B × Q 9 B-K2 0-0 10 0-0 P-KR3 11 B-Q2 N-N3 12 B-R5 B-K3 13 N-B3 KR-K1 14 B × N RP × B 15 N-Q4 B-Q4 16 N × B N × N 17 B-B3 P-QB3 18 B × N P × B 19 N-B5 QR-B1 20 QR-K1 B-B1 21 R × R R × R 22 P-Q4 R-K7 23 N-K3 R-Q7 24 N × P R × BP 25 R-N1 R-Q7 26 N × P R × QP 27 N-Q7 R-Q7 28 K-B1 P-Q4 39 K-K1 R-B7 30 N × B K × N 31 R-Q1 R × NP 32 P-QR4 R-R7 33 R × P R × RP 34 R-Q8ch K-K2 35 R-Q3 P-QN4 36 R-K3ch K-Q3 37 R-Q3ch K-B3 38 R-B3ch K-N3 39 R-B1 R-K5ch 40 K-Q2 P-N5 41 P-B3 R-K4 42 R-B4 R-QN4 43 P-N3 P-N5 44 R-B8 K-N2 45 R-B8 P-N7 46 R × Pch K-N3 47 R × P P-N8 = Q 48 R-Q7 Q-R7ch 49 K-Q3 Q × P White resigns.

White: DUCHESS
Black: BLACK KNIGHT

Sicilian Defence

1 P-K4 P-QB4 2 P-Q4 P × P 3 P-QB3 P × P 4 N × P N-QB3 5 N-B3 P-Q3 6 B-QB4 P-K3 7 0-0 N-B3 8 Q-K2 B-K2 9 R-Q1 P-K4 10 B-K3 N-KN5 11 B-Q2 B-R5 12 B-K1 B-K2 13 B-Q2 B-K3 14 B × B P × B 15 N-KN5 B × N 16 Q × N B × B 17 Q × NP R-KB1 18 Q × NP Q-N3 19 Q × Rch K-K2 20 Q × Rch K × Q 21 R × B Q-B2 22 R(R1)-Q1 N-Q5 23 P-B4 Q-KN2 24 R-Q3 P-KR4 25 K-R1 P-R3 26 P × P P × P 37 R-KB1ch K-K1 38 R-N3 Q-K2 29 R-N8ch K-Q2 30 R-QR8 K-B3 31 R × Pch K-N2 32 R-R4 K-B3 33 R-R5 Q-N5 34 R × P Q × P 35 R-QB5ch K-Q3 36 P-K5ch K-K2 37 R-QN1 Q-KB7 38 B-B7ch K-Q1 39 R-KR7 N-B3 40 R-R8ch K-B2 41 N-N5ch K-Q2 42 R-R7ch K-Q1 43 N-Q6 Q-B1 44 K-N1 P-R5 45 R(N1)-N7 N-K2 46 R-N8ch K-B2 47 R × Q P-R6 48 R × Nch K-B3 49 P × P K-Q4 50 N-B7 K-Q5 51 R × P K-Q4

52 R-Q6ch K-K5 53 R-B8 K-B6 54 R-B4 K-K7 55 R-K4ch K-B6 56 N-N5mate.

White: OSTRICH
Black: BRUTE FORCE

Centre Counter

1 P-K4 P-Q4 2 P×P Q×P 3 N-QB3 Q-K4ch 4 KN-K2 P-QR4 5 P-Q4 Q-KB4 6 B-K3 P-KN4 7 N-N3 Q-N3 8 B-Q3 P-KB4 9 0-0 N-KB3 10 N-N5 K-Q1 11 P-Q5 P-N5 12 B-Q4 P-K3 13 P×P B-N5 14 B×P K-K2 15 B×Q P×B 16 B×Nch K×B 17 Q-Q4ch K-K2 18 Q-N7ch K×P 19 N×Pch K-Q3 20 N×R R-K1 21 Q-QB7ch K-K3 22 KR-K1ch B×R 23 R×Bch K-B3 24 R×R B-Q2 25 Q-K5ch K-B2 26 Q-K7mate.

White: XENARBOR
Black: CHESS 4.6

Bononi Defence

1 P-Q4 N-KB3 2 P-QB4 P-B4 3 P-Q5 P-K3 4 N-KB3 P×P 5 P×P P-Q3 6 P-K3 B-B4 7 N-B3 QN-Q2 8 P-KN3 N-K4 9 N×N P×N 10 Q-N3 Q-N3 11 Q×Q P×Q 12 B-N2 B-Q6 13 P-K4 B-Q3 14 B-K3 0-0 15 0-0-0 B-B5 16 P-N3 B-R3 17 N-R4 B-N4 18 N×NP R-R3 19 P-QR4 B-K7 20 R-Q2 R×N 21 R×B R×P 22 R-B2 R-B1 23 B-R3 R-R1 24 R-B4 P-QN4 25 R-QN4 25 R-B2 R×P 26 B-N2 P-B5 27 P-R4 P-B6 28 R-K2 N×KP 29 B×N R×B 30 R-QR2 R-R6 31 R×R B×Rch 32 K-B2 B-N5 33 R-R1 P-B4 34 R-R8ch K-B2 35 R-QN8 P-B5 36 K-Q3 P×B 37 P×P R-QB5 38 R×P P-B7 39 K×R B-K2 40 P-K4 P-B8=Qch 41 K-Q3 Q-B8ch 42 K-K3 Q×R 43 P-N4 B×P 44 K-Q2 Q-B5 45 P-Q6 Q×P 46 P-N5 B×Pch 47 K-B3 P-R4 48 K-N3 P-R5 49 K-R2 Q-QN5 50 K-R1 B-B8 51 K-R2 Q-N7mate.

Round 3

White: CHESS 4.6
Black: CHAOS

Sicilian Defence

1 P-K4 P-QB4 2 N-KB3 N-QB3 3 B-N5 N-B3 4 P-K5 N-Q4 5 0-0 P-K3 6 B×N QP×B 7 P-Q3 B-K2 8 N-R3 0-0 9 B×Q2 B-Q2 10 Q-K2 Q-N3 11 N-B4 Q-Q1 12 N-Q6 Q-N3 13 P-B4 Q×P 15 P×N BP×P 15 KR-N1 Q-R6 16 R×P Q-R5 17 R-QB1 QR-N1 18 R-B7 R-N7 19 R(B7)×BP KR-N1 20 Q-K3 Q×P 21 R-B7 B×N 22 R×B B-R6 23 Q-B4 P-B4 24 P×Pe.p. B-B1 25 P×P B-K2 26 R×B P-KR3 27 Q-B7ch K-R2 28 P-N8=Qmate.

White: TYRO
Black: CHUTE

Queen's Gambit Declined

1 P-Q4 P-Q4 2 P-QB4 P-K3 3 P-KN3 P×P 4 N-KB3 N-QB3 5 P-QR3 N-B3 6 N-B3 P-QR3 7 P-K4 P-QN4 8 B-B4 N-KR4 9 B-R3 N×B 10 P×N Q-B3 11 Q-Q2 Q-R3 12 N-N5 N-Q1 13 P-Q5 B-K2 14 B-N4 P-KB4 15 KP×P P×BP 16 B-B3 B-N2 17 0-0 Q-N3 18 QR-K1 P-R3 19 Q-K3 Q-KB3 20 N-K6 R-QB1 21 N×N K×N 22 B-R5 P-N4 23 K-R1 P×P 24 Q×P B-Q3 25 Q-B3 R-KN1 26 R-KN1 R×Rch 27 R×R Q-K4 28 Q-N2 K-Q2 29 R-Q1 B-B4 30 R-Q2 Q-K8ch 31 Q-NQ×R 32 Q-N7ch B-K2 33 Q-K5 Q×BP 34 Q-K6ch K-Q1 35 Q×KRP Q-B8mate.

White: BLACK KNIGHT
Black: XENARBOR

Sicilian Defence

1 P-K4 P-QB4 2 N-KB3 N-QB3 3 N-B3 P-Q3 4 P×Q4 P×P 5 N×P N×N 6 Q×N N-B3 7 P-K5 P×P 7 Q×KP P-QR3 9 B-K2 Q-Q3 10 Q×Q P×Q 11 B-KN5 B-K3 12 B×N P×B 13 B-B3 0-0-0 14 0-0-0 B-R3ch 15 K-N1 B-N2 16 R-Q3 P-B4 17 KR-Q1 B-K4 18 B-Q5 B×B 19 N×B B×RP 20 R-KR3 B-K4 21 P-KB4 P-KR4 22 P×B P×P 23 R-KB3 P-B5 24 P-KN3 P×P 25 R×NP P-R5 26 R-N7 P-B4 27 N-N6ch K-N1 28 R(Q1)-Q7 R×R 29 N×Rch K-R2 30 N×P R-K1 31 N-B6ch K-R1 32 N-K7 P-B5 33 R-N8 R×R 34 P-B4 R-N8ch 35 K-B2 P-B6 36 N-B8 K-N1 37 N-N6 P-B7 38 N-Q7ch K-R2 39 N-K5 P-B8=Q 40 K-B3 P-R6 41 P-B5 P-R7 42 P-R4 P-R8=Q 43 P-N4 Q-R8ch 44 K-Q3 Q×N 45 P-R5 Q(R8)-K5ch 46 K-Q2 Q(K4)-Q5mate.

White: BLITZ V
Black: 8080 CHESS

King Pawn Opening

1 P-K4 P-K4 2 N-KB3 P-Q4 3 N×P P×P 4 B-B4 N-KR3 5 0-0 N-B3 6 N×N P×N 7 Q-K2 B-KB4 8 P-Q3 B-B4 9 B×N P×B 10 Q-R5 Q-B3 11 P×P Q×P 12 Q×BPch K-Q1 13 Q×B B×Pch 14 Q×B Q×R 15 Q-R4ch K-Q2 16 R-Q1ch K-K1 17 Q-R5 ch Resigns.

White: OSTRICH
Black: DUCHESS

Petroff Defence

1 P-K4 P-K4 2 N-KB3 N-KB3 3 B-B4 N×P 4 Q-K2 P-Q4 5 N×P B-K3 6 0-0 B-Q3 7 N-KB3 0-0 8 P-Q3 P×B 9 P×N N-B3 10 N-N5 N-Q5 11 Q-R5 P-KR3 12 N×B P×N 13 Q-Q1 P-B4 14 P-QB3 N-B3 15 N-R3 Q-N1 16 P-R4 N-K4 17 B-K3 B-K2 18 P-B4 N-Q6 19 N×P N×BP 20 P-KN3 N-N3 21 Q-N4 K-R2 22 P-R5 N-K4 23 R×R N×Q 24 R×Q R×R 25 B-B4 R-Q1 26 N-K5 N×N 27 B×N B-B3 28 B×B P×B 29 R-KB1 K-N2 30 K-N2 K-B2 31 K-B3 R-Q6ch 32 K-N4 R-Q7 33 R-QN1 R-KB7 34 P-R4 K-K2 35 P-N4 P-B5

36 R-K1 R-B7 37 R-K3 P-N3 38 P-R5 P × P 39 P × P K-Q3 40 K-B4 R-QR7 41 R-B3 R × P 42 K-K3 K-K4 43 R-B2 R-R8 44 R-B2 R-K8ch 45 K-Q2 R × P 46 R-B1 R-N5 47 R-K1ch K-Q4 White resigns.

White: BRUTE FORCE
Black: WITA

Queen Pawn Opening

1 P-Q4 N-KB3 2 N-QB3 N-B3 3 P-Q5 N × P 4 Q × N P-Q3 5 P-QR3 P-K3 6 Q-Q2 B-K2 7 P-QN4 B-B3 8 P-N5 N-K4 9 P-B4 N-N5 10 N-B3 P-B3 11 P × P P × P 12 P-R3 B-R5ch 13 K-Q1 N-B7ch 14 K-K1 N × Rch 15 P-N2 N × P 16 Q-Q3 Q-B3 17 N × B Q × N 18 Q-B3 P-Q4 19 Q-N4 Q × Q 20 P × Q N × B 21 K × N P-QR3 22 B-K3 P-K4 23 P × P B × P 24 P-R4 P-KR4 25 P-R5 26 R-R4 B-K3 27 B-B2 P-R6 28 P-K3 P-R7 29 B-N3 P-R8 = Qch 30 K-K2 Q-QB8 31 K-Q3 R-QN1 32 P-K4 R-N7 33 R-R3 R × P R × P 34 N-R2 Q-Q7mate.

Round 4

White: WITA
Black: BLACK KNIGHT

Sicilian Defence

1 P-K4 P-QB4 2 N-KB3 N-QB3 3 P-Q4 P × P 4 N × P N-B3 5 N-QB3 P-Q3 6 P-KR3 P-QR3 7 P-KN4 N × N 8 Q × N P-K4 9 Q-Q3 B-K3 10 B-N2 B-K2 11 B-K3 R-QB1 12 Q-Q2 P-KR4 13 P-N5 N-Q2 14 N-Q5 B × N 15 P × B R-B5 16 Q-K2 P-N4 17 P-N3 R-KR5 18 P-KB4 0-0 19 0-0 P × P 20 B-B2 P-B6 21 Q × BP B × P 22 B × R B × B 23 Q × RP B-B3 24 QR-K1 B-B6 25 P-R3 Q-N3ch 26 K-R2 N-B3 27 Q-Q1 B × R 28 R × B R-B1 29 R-K2 R-B6 30 Q-Q2 Q-R4 31 R-K3 R × NP 32 Q × Q R × R 33 P-QR4 R-K7 34 Q × RP R × P 35 Q-R8ch K-R2 36 P × P R-N7 37 Q-B6 N-K5 38 Q-K8 N-N4 39 Q-K7 K-R3 40 P-N6 P-B4 41 Q-K3 K-N3 42 P-R4 N-K5 43 K-N1 R-N8ch 44 Q-K1 R × Qch 45 K-R2 R-QN8 46 B-B1 R × B 47 P-N7 R-QN8 48 P-N8 = Q R × Q 49 K-N1 N-B6 50 P-R5ch K × P 51 K-R2 P-N4 52 K-N3 P-N5 53 K-N2 P-B5 54 K-B2 R-N8 55 K-N2 N-K5 56 K-R2 K-R5 57 K-N2 P-B6ch 58 K-R2 P-N6mate.

White: DUCHESS
Black: CHESS 4.6

Sicilian Defence

1 P-K4 P-QB4 2 P-Q4 P×P 3 P-PB● P×P 4 N×P N-QB3 5 N-B3 P-Q3 6 B-Q4 P-K3 7 0-0 N-B3 8 Q-K2 B-K2 9 R-Q1 P-K4 10 B-K3 N-KN5 11 B-Q2 N-K5 12 N×N P×N 13 N-N5 Q-N3 14 B-B4 N-K4 15 N×P(Q4) N×B 16 Q×N B-N5 17 Q-R4ch B-Q2 18 Q-N3 0-0 19 Q×Q P×Q 20 P-QR3 KR-B1 21 QR-B1 R×R 22 R×R R-R5 23 B-K3 B-Q1 24 P-B3 R-R4 25 R-Q1 B-KB3 26 R-Q2 R-QB4 27 N-K2 R-B3 28 P-QR4 B-K3 29 N-Q4 R-B8ch 30 K-B2 B-Q2 31 N-N5 B×N 32 P×B R-QN8 33 B×P R×P 34 R×R B×R 35 K-K3 K-B1 36 B-Q4 B×Bch 37 K×B K-K1 38 K-Q5 K-Q2 39 P-N6 P-N3 40 P-B4 K-K2 41 P-R3 P-B3 42 P-R4 K-Q2 43 P-N4 P-R3 44 P-R5 P×P 46 P×P K-K2 46 K-Q4 K-K3 47 K-B4 K-K2 48 P-B5 K-Q1 49 K-N4 K-Q2 50 K-N5 K-K1 51 K-R4 K-K2 52 K-N4 K-Q1 53 K-B4 K-K1 54 K-Q4 K-Q2 55 K-Q5 K-K2 56 K-Q4 K-K1 57 K-B4 K-B2 Adjudicated drawn.

White: BRUTE FORCE
Black: 8080 CHESS

Queen Pawn Opening

1 P-Q4 P-Q4 2 N-QB3 N-QB 3 B-B4 N-B3 4 N-N5 P-K4 5 B×P B-N5ch 6 P-QB3 N×B 7 P×N B×Pch 8 N×B N-K5 9 N×N P×N 1- Q-R4ch B-Q2 11 Q×KP P-QN4 12 P[KN4 0-0 13 B-N2 P-QB3 14 P-KR4 P-QR4 15 0-0-0 R-R3 16 Q-Q4 P-KB4 17 Q×B Q×Q 18 R×Q P×P 19 R-Q6 R×P 20 B×P R-B4 21 B-Q5ch K-B1 22 R×R R×P 23 P-K4 P-R5 24 R-QN6 P-N4 25 P×P K-N2 26 R-N7ch K-N3 27 R(R1)×P K×P 28 R×P K-B5 29 R-QR5 P-R6 30 R-KB7ch K-K6 31 R×Pch K-Q5 32 R-KN7 K-B4 33 R×P K-Q3 34 R-R6ch K-B4 35 N-B3 R-K2 36 R-QB6ch K-N5 37 P-K5ch K-N4 38 N-Q4ch K-R4 39 N-N3ch Resigns.

White: CHUTE
Black: XENARBOR

Sicilian Defence

1 P-K4 P-QB4 2 P-QB4 N-QB3 3 N-KB3 P-K4 4 N-B3 N-B3 5 B-K2 P-Q3 6 0-0 P-KN3 7 P-Q3 B-N2 8 B-N5 N-Q5 9 N×N BP×N 10 N-Q5 P-KR3 11 N×Nch B×N 12 B×B Q×B 13 Q-R4ch B-Q2 14 Q-R5 P-N3 15 Q-Q5 R-QN1 16 QR-B1 P-QR4 17 P-QN3 P-R4 18 B-B3 P-KR5 19 P-R4 P-R6 20 KR-K1 R-QB1 21 Q-N7 Q-Q1 22 Q-R7 B-B3 23 P×P R-R1 24 Q×R Q×Q 25 B-N4 P-KN4 26 R-B2 Q-Q1 27 R(B2)-K2 Q-K2 28 P-B3 Q-B3 29 K-N2 Q-B5 30 B-B5 0-0 31 B-N4 P-B3 32 B-K6ch K-R1 33 B-B5 R-KN1 34 B-N4 R-K1 35 B-R5 R-KN1 36 B-N4 R-N2 37 B-B8 R-KR2 38 B-B5 R-R5 39 B-N4 R-R2 40 B-B5 R-R3 41 B-N4 R-R5 42 B-B5 R-R4 43 B-N4 R-R3 44 B-K6 R-R2 45 B-B5 R-KN2 46 B-N4 Drawn by repetition of moves.

White: CHAOS
Black: BLITZ

Queen's Gambit Declined

1 P-Q4 P-Q4 2 P-QB4 P-K3 3 N-QB3 N-KB3 4 B-N5 B-K2 5 P-K3 0-0 6 N-B3 P-KR3 7 B-R4 N-K5 8 B × B Q × B 9 P × P N × N 10 P × N P × P 11 Q-N3 R-Q1 12 B-Q3 N-B3 13 0-0 R-Q3 14 KR-B1 P-QN3 15 P-B4 P × P 16 Q × BP B-N5 17 N-Q2 QR-Q1 18 B-K4 B-Q2 19 QR-N1 P-QR4 20 B-Q5 N-N5 21 B × Pch Q × B 22 Q × P B-K3 23 P-QR3 Q × Q 24 R × Q N-Q4 25 R(B7)-B1 R-QB1 26 R × Rch B × R 27 R-QB1 B-N2 28 P-N3 P-QN4 29 N-N3 P-R5 30 N-B5 B-B3 31 P-K4 N-N3 32 P-Q5 B-K1 33 N-N7 R-Q2 34 N-B5 R-QB2 35 R-B3 B-N3 36 P-B4 N-B5 37 N-R6 R-K2 38 P-K5 B-K5 39 P-Q6 R-KB2 40 N-B7 B-B3 41 P-K6 R-B1 42 P-K7 R-B1 43 R-Q3 B-Q2 44 N-R6 K-B2 45 K-B2 K-K1 46 N-B7ch R × N 47 P × R K × P 48 K-B3 B-B4 49 R-Q5 B-N5ch 50 K × B N-Q3 51 R × N Resigns.

White: TYRO
Black: OSTRICH

Queen's Gambit Accepted

1 P-Q4 P-Q4 2 P-QB4 P × P 3 P-K4 N-QB3 4 P-Q5 N-K4 5 P-B4 B-N5 6 N-KB3 B × N 7 P × B N-Q6ch 8 B × N P × B 9 Q × P P-QB3 10 K-K2 Q-Q2 11 P × P Q × Qch 12 K × Q 0-0-0ch 13 K-K2 P × P 14 R-Q1 R-Q3 15 B-K3 R-R3 16 B × P R × Pch 17 B-B2 P-R4 18 P-N3 R-R3 19 P-R4 R-B3 20 K-K3 R-R6 21 P-N4 P-K4 22 P × P R(B3) × Pch 23 K-K2 B × P 24 B-N6 N-K2 25 R-Q4 R-K6ch 26 K-B2 B-K8ch 27 K-B1 R(R6)-B6ch 28 K-N1 R-K7 29 R-Q8ch K-N2 30 B-Q4 R × P 31 R-Q7ch K-B1 32 R × N R-N5ch 33 K-R2 R × B 34 K-N2 R-B7ch 35 K-N3 R-Q6ch 36 K-R4 R-B4mate.

Second World Computer Championship

Note that the round one game between Duchess and Kaissa will be found on page 69.

Round 1

White: CHESS 4.6
Black: BCP

Scotch Gambit

1 P-K4 P-K4 2 N-KB3 N-QB3 3 P-Q4 P × P 4 P-B3 Q-K2 5 P × P Q × Pch 6 B-K2 P-Q4 7 N-B3 B-QN5 8 0-0 B × N 9 B-Q3 Q-K2 10 P × B N-B3 11 Q-N3 N-K5 12 R-K1 Q-K3 13 N-N5 Q-Q2 14 P-B3 P-B4 15 P × N BP × P 16 B × P P × B 17 R × Pch N-K2 18 Q-B7ch K-Q1 19 Q × P Q-K1 20 N-B7ch K-Q2 21 N × R K-Q3 22 R × N Q × R 23 B-R3ch K-B3 24 Q × Q P-KR4 25 Q-B5ch K-Q2 26 R-K1 P-R3 27 Q-Q5mate.

White: CHUTE
Black: MASTER

Pirc Defence

1 P-K4 P-Q3 2 N-QB3 P-KN3 3 B-B4 B-K3 4 B×B P×B 5 N-B3 N-QB3 6
Q-K2 B-N2 7 0-0 Q-Q2 8 P-QR3 0-0-0 9 P-QN3 P-Q4 10 P×P P×P 11 R-
R2 P-Q5 12 N-Q1 P-Q6 13 P×P Q-Q4 14 B-N2 P-K4 15 R-K1 Q×NP 16 N-
B3 N-Q5 17 Q-K4 N×Nch 18 Q×N N-R3 19 Q-K3 R-Q5 20 B-R1 N-N5 21
Q-R3 K-N1 22 R-K4 P-KR4 23 Q-N3 Q-K3 24 P-R3 N-R3 25 P-B4 N-B4 26
Q-B3 N-Q3 27 R×R P×R 28 N-Q5 P-B3 29 N-N4 Q-K8ch 30 Q-B1 R-K1
31 Q×Q R×Qch 32 K-B2 R-R8 33 P-QR4 K-B2 34 N-B2 P-B4 35 N-K1 N-
B4 36 R-B2 K-Q3 37 R-N2 P-N3 38 R-N1 P-R5 39 R-B1 N-N6 40 K-B3 R-
B8ch 41 K-N4 N-K7 42 R-N1 B-B3 43 P-N3 P×P 44 P-R4 P-N7 46 B×P
Adjudicated a win for Black.

White: CHAOS
Black: BS 66/76

Albin Counter Gambit

1 P-Q4 P-Q4 2 P-QB4 P-K4 3 QP×P P-Q5 4 N-KB3 N-QB3 5 QN-Q2 B-K3
6 P-KN3 P-KR4 7 B-N2 P-Q6 8 0-0 R-N1 9 P×P Q×P 10 Q-N3 Q-Q1 11 N-
K4 N-Q5 12 N×N Q×N 13 B-K3 R-Q1 14 B×Q R×B 15 Q×P B×P 16
KR-Q1 B-Q6 17 Q-N8ch K-Q2 18 Q×B P-QB4 19 R×B K-B2 20
Q×QBPch K-N1 21 Q-KB8ch K-B2 22 R×R N-K2 23 Q×Nch K-N3 24 Q-
N4ch Black lost on time.

White: BELLE
Black: BLACK KNIGHT

Sicilian Defence

1 P-K4 P-QB4 2 N-KB3 N-QB3 3 P-Q4 P×P 4 N×P N-B3 5 N-QB3 P-Q3 6
B-QN5 B-Q2 7 0-0 N×N 8 Q×N B×B 9 N×B P-K4 10 Q-R4 N-Q2 11 R-
Q1 P-QR3 12 N×Pch B×N 13 R×B Q-B2 14 R-Q3 P-QN4 15 Q-N3 0-0 16
B-N5 N-B4 17 Q-B3 R-R2 18 B-Q8 R×B 19 Q×N R×R 20 Q×Q R×Q
21 P×R R-B7 22 P-QN3 P-QR4 23 P-B3 P-B3 24 P-QR4 P-N5 25 P-B4 R-
B6 26 P×P P×P 27 R-N1 R×QP 28 K-B2 P-N4 29 R-N2 P-R4 30 K-K2 R-
QB6 31 R-N1 R-B7ch 32 K-B1 R-Q7 33 R-B1 R-N7 34 R-B8ch K-N2 35 R-
B7ch K-B3 36 R-B6ch K-B2 37 R-B5 R-N8ch 38 K-B2 Adjudicated drawn.

White: OSTRICH
Black: WITA

Sicilian Defence

1 P-K4 P-QB4 2 N-KB3 P-Q3 3 B-B4 N-KB3 4 N-QB3 P-K3 5 0-0 B-K2 6 P-
Q3 B-Q2 7 B-K3 N-B3 8 B-QN5 0-0 9 N-N5 P-KR3 10 B×N B×B 11 N-R3
K-R1 12 Q-B3 N-Q2 12 KR-N1 Q-R4 14 Q-N4 B-B3 15 B-Q2 B-Q5 16 Q-

R4 Q-Q1 17 Q×Q QR×Q 18 N-K2 P-B4 19 N×B P×N 20 N-B4 QR-K1 21 N-K2 P-K4 22 P×P R×P 23 P-KB4 N-B4 24 B-N4 P-KN3 25 P×P R(B4)×P 26 N×P B-Q4 27 P-B4 N×P 28 B×P R-K5 29 N-N5 B×P 30 N×P R-QR1 31 P-QN3 B-R3 32 P-QN4 R×N 33 P-N5 P-N3 34 P×B R×P 35 B-B7 N-N5 36 P-QR3 N-B7 37 R-R2 R-K8ch 38 R×R N×R 39 K-B2 N-Q6ch 40 K-B3 N-N5 41 R-N2 N-Q4 42 B-Q6 P-QN4 43 B-B5 R-KB3 ch 44 K-K4 N-B2 45 R-KB2 N-K1 46 R×R N×Rch 47 K-Q3 K-N2 48 B-Q4 K-B2 49 B×N K×B 50 K-Q4 K-K2 51 K-B5 K-Q1 52 K×P K-B2 53 P-QR4 P-N4 54 P-R5 K-N1 55 K-N6 K-B1 56 P-R6 K-N1 57 P-N4 K-R1 58 P-R7 P-R4 59 P×P P-N5 60 P-R6 P-N6 61 P-R7 Resigns.

White: ELSA
Black: BLITZ V
Queen's Gambit Declined
1 P-Q4 P-Q4 2 P-QB4 P-K3 3 N-QB3 N-KB3 4 B-N5 B0K2 5 N-B3 0-0 6 Q-N3 P×P 7 Q×BP QN-Q2 8 0-0-0 N-N3 9 Q-Q3 B-Q2 10 N-K5 R-B1 11 Q-B3 N(B3)-Q4 12 B×B Q×B 13 N×B Q×N 14 P-K4 N×N 15 Q×N Q-R5 16 P-QR3 KR-Q1 17 Q-B5 R-Q3 18 B-N5 Q-R4 19 P-B4 P-QR3 20 B-K8 Q×Qch 21 P×Q R×Rch 22 R×R R×B 23 P×N P×P 24 P-QN4 P-R3 25 K-N2 R-K2 26 R-Q6 P-QN4 27 P-N4 R-B2 28 K-N3 K-B1 29 P-K5 R-B5 30 R-Q8ch K-K2 31 R-QN8 R-B2 32 P-KR4 P-KN3 33 P-N5 P-KR4 34 R-QR8 K-Q2 35 R-QN8 K-B3 36 R-Q8 R-Q2 37 R×R K×R 38 K-B3 K39 K-Q4 P-N3 40 K-K4 P-R4 41 K-Q4 P-R5 42 K-K4 K-Q2 43 K-Q4 K-B3 44 K-K4 K-B1 45 K-Q4 K-K1 Adjudicated drawn.

White: TELL
Black: DARK HORSE
Akekhine Defence
1 P-K4 N-KB3 2 N-QB3 N-B3 3 P-Q4 P-Q3 4 B-QN5 B-Q2 5 B-N5 P-K4 6 B×KN Q×B 7 N-Q5 Q-Q1 8 N-KB3 P×P 9 N×QP B-K2 10 B×N B×B 11 N×QB P×N 12 N-N4 Q-Q2 13 Q-Q4 B-B3 14 Q-K3 B×P 15 R-QN1 B-B3 16 N-QR6 0-0 17 R-N7 KR-B1 18 R×RP Q-N5 19 0-0 R×R 20 Q×R Q×KP 21 Q-N7 R-B1 22 Q×P(B7) B-K4 23 R-Q1 Q-K7 24 R-N1 Q×N 25 R-N8 P-N3 26 R×Rch K×R 27 P-N3 Q-B5 28 Q-Q8ch K-N2 29 P-B4 B-Q5ch 30 K-N2 Q×BPch 31 K-B3 Q-B7ch 32 K-N4 Q×KRP 33 Q-R5 P-KB4ch 34 Q×P P×Qch 35 K×P Q×NP 36 K-K4 P-B4 37 P-R4 Q-N7ch 38 K-Q3 Q-B6ch 39 K-B4 Q×P 40 P-R5 Q-KB8ch 41 K-Q5 B-K4 42 P-R6 Q-B6ch 43 K-B4 Q-K7ch 44 K-Q5 Q×P 45 K-K4 Q-K7ch 46 K-Q5 Q-B6ch 47 K-B4 B-Q5 48 K-N5 Q-N2ch 49 K-B4 P-R3 50 K-Q3 Q-QN7 52 K-B4 B-K4 52 K-Q5 Adjudicated a win for Black.

Round 2

White: KAISSA
Black: TELL

Ruy Lopez

1 P-K4 P-K4 2 N-KB3 N-QB3 3 B-N5 N-B3 4 0-0 N×P 5 P-Q4 N×QP 6 N×N P×N 7 Q×P N-B4 8 R-K1ch N-K3 9 N-B3 P-QB4 10 Q-K5 P-KR4 11 N-Q5 B-K2 12 B-N5 Q-R4 13 B×B P-R3 14 Q×NP R-R3 15 Q-N8ch N-B1 16 Q×Nmate.

White: MASTER
Black: CHESS 4.6

Reti Opening

1 N-KB3 P-Q4 2 P-B4 P×P 3 N-R3 P-K3 4 Q-R4ch B-Q2 5 Q×BP N-QB3 6 P-K3 N-B3 7 B-Q3 P-QR3 8 N-B2 P-QN4 9 Q-B4 B-Q3 10 Q-N5 0-0 11 0-0 P-K4 12 Q-R4 Q-K2 13 B-K4 N×B 14 Q×N K-R1 15 P-KN4 N-R4 16 P-N5 B-B3 17 Q-KN4 B×N 18 Q×B Q×Pch 19 Q-N2 Q×Qch 20 K×Q P-K5 21 P-B3 P×Pch 22 R×P P-KB4 23 P-N3 N-B3 24 B-N2 N-K4 25 B×N B×B 26 R(R1)-KB1 P-N3 27 P-KR3 P-B4 28 P-Q4 P×P 29 P×P B-Q3 30 N-K3 R(B1)-K1 31 R(B1)-B2 R(R1)-Q1 32 R-Q2 B-N5 33 R-Q3 B-B1 34 P-Q5 R-K4 35 P-QR4 P×P 36 P×P B-QB4 37 P-Q6 B×P 38 N-B4 R-K3 39 N×B R(K3)×N 40 R×R R×R 41 R-QB3 R-Q5 White resigns.

White: DARK HORSE
Black: CHAOS

Three Knights

1 N-QB3 P-K4 2 N-B3 N-QB3 3 P-K4 B-N5 4 N-Q5 N-B3 5 N×B N×N 6 P-B3 N-B3 7 Q-K2 0-0 8 P-Q4 P-Q3 9 P-QN3 B-N5 10 P-Q5 N-K2 11 P-N3 P-B3 12 P×P P×P 13 B-N5 Q-R4 14 Q-K3 N(B3)-Q4 15 P×N N×P 16 Q-Q2 B×N 17 P-QN4 Q-R6 18 R-KN1 Q×BP 19 Q×Q N×Q 20 B-K7 KR-K1 21 B×P N-K5 22 B-B5 N×B 23 P×N QR-Q1 24 B-K2 B×B 25 K×B R-Q4 26 QR-QB1 R(K1)-Q1 27 KR-Q1 R×R 28 R×R R-K1 29 R-Q6 R-QB1 30 K-B3 P-QR4 31 K-K4 P-B3 32 K-B3 P-R5 33 R-Q7 R-R1 34 R-Q6 R-R3 35 K-N2 P-R3 36 P-R4 K-B2 37 P-R5 K-N1 38 P-B3 K-B1 39 R-Q8ch K-K2 40 R-Q6 K-B1 41 R-Q8ch K-K2 42 R-Q6 K-K1 43 P-R3 K-K2 44 K-B2 K-B1 45 R-Q8ch K-K2 46 R-Q6 K-B1 47 R-Q8ch K-B2 48 R-Q7ch K-N1 49 R-Q8ch K-R2 50 R-QB8 P-N4 51 P×Pe.p.ch K×P 52 R-KN8ch K-B2 53 R-QB8 K-K3 54 R-K8ch K-B2 55 R-QB8 K-N3 56 R-KN8ch K-R4 57 P-N4ch K-R5 58 R-N6 P-R4 59 P×P K×P 60 R×P K-N4 61 R-K6 K-B4 62 R-R6 K-N4 63 R-Q6 K-B5 64 R-N6 K-B4 65 R-N4 R-R4 66 R-QB4 K-K3 67 K-K2 K-Q4 68 R-K4 R×P 69 R×RP R-B6 70 R-R7 P-B4 Adjudicated drawn.

White: BLACK KNIGHT
Black: ELSA

Ruy Lopez

1 P-K4 P-K4 2 N-NB3 N-QB3 3 B-N5 P-Q3 4 P-Q4 P×P 5 Q×P B-Q2 6
B×N B×B 7 N-B3 Q-B3 8 B-K3 B-K2 9 N-Q5 Q×Q 10 N×Q B×N 11
P×B 0-0-0 12 N-N5 P-QR3 13 N-R7ch K-N1 14 0-0-0 N-B3 15 P-KB3 KR-
K1 16 KR-K1 B-B1 17 R-Q2 R×B 18 R×R K×N 19 R-Q1 R-Q2 20 P-QB4
P-QN4 21 P×P P×P 22 R-N3 K-R3 23 R-R3ch K-N3 24 R-N3 P-N3 25 P-
QR4 B-R3ch 26 K-N1 K-R4 37 R×Pch K×P 28 R-N7 R-K2 29 R-Q3 R-
K8ch 30 K-R2 R-K6 31 R-Q4ch K-R4 32 R×P B-N4 33 P-R4 N-K1 34 R×P
B-B3 35 R-K4 R×R 36 P×R B×RP 37 R×P Adjudicated a draw.

White: DUCHESS
Black: OSTRICH

Petroff Defence

1 P-K4 P-K4 2 N-KB3 N-KB3 3 P-Q4 B-K2 4 P×P N×P 5 B-Q3 P-Q4 6
P×Pe.p. N×QP 7 0-0 0-0 8 R-K1 B-N5 9 P-B3 K-R1 10 B-KB4 N-B3 11
QN-Q2 P-KN4 12 B-K3 N-B4 13 Q-K2 B×N 14 N×B N×B 15 Q×N P-N5
16 B-B5 R-KN1 17 N-K5 N×N 18 Q×Qch B-B3 19 Q-B4 B-N4 20 Q-K4 B-
Q7 21 QR-Q1 Q-N4 22 R-K2 B-B5 23 R-Q7 QR-K1 24 Q×R R×Q 25
R×Rch K-N2 26 B-K6 P-QR4 27 R×KBPch K-R3 28 R(K8)-K7 Q-N3 29
B-B5 Q-N1 30 B-K4 Q-Q1 31 R-K6ch K-N4 32 R-B5ch K-R5 33 R-KR6ch
Resigns.

White: BLITZ V
Black: BELLE

Ruy Lopez

1 P-K4 P-K4 2 N-KB3 N-QB3 3 B-N5 N-B3 4 0-0 N×P 5 R-K1 N-Q3 6
N×P B-K2 7 B×N QP×B 8 N-QB3 0-0 9 Q-R5 R-K1 10 P-Q4 B-K3 11 B-
B4 N-N4 12 N×N P×N 13 N-B3 Q-Q2 14 R-K3 P-R4 15 P-KR3 P-R5 16 B-
K5 Q-B3 17 P-B3 P-R3 18 P-R3 QR-Q1 19 N-Q2 B-N4 20 R-K2 P-KN3 21
Q-B3 Q×Q 22 N×Q B-QB5 23 R(K2)-K1 P-QB3 24 N×B P×N 25 B-B6
R-QB1 26 B×P R-R1 27 R-K7 R×R 28 B×R R-K1 29 R-K1 B-N6 30 R-
K5 B-R7 31 P-KB4 B-K3 32 B-B6 R-KB1 33 P-R4 B-N5 34 R-K7 B-B1 35 P-
KN3 K-R2 36 K-N2 K-N1 37 K-B3 P-N3 38 K-K4 B-B4ch 39 K-K3 R-B1 40
KB3 R-N1 41 R-K5 B-B7 42 P-Q5 P×P 43 R×P P-N5 44 RP×P R-K1 45
R-Q6 B-K5ch 46 K-K3 P-QN4 47 R-Q4 B-B3ch 48 B-K5 B-N7 49 K-B2 B-
B3 50 K-K2 B-N7 51 K-K3 P-B3 52 R-Q6 P×B 53 R×Pch K-B2 54 P-B5 B-
R6 55 P-N4 R-KN1 56 R×R K×R 57 K-B3 P-K5 ch 58 K-B4 P-K6 59 K×P
B×P 60 K-K4 K-N2 61 K-B4 B-K7 62 K-N5 B-Q8 63 P-B6 ch K-R2 64 P-B4
P×P 65 P-N5 P-B6 66 P×P P-R6 67 P-B7 K-N2 68 P-B8=Qch K×Q White
resigns.

White: BCP
Black: WITA

Sicilian Defence

1 P-K4 P-QB4 2 N-QB3 P-Q3 3 P-Q4 N-KB3 4 B-K3 P-K3 5 N-B3 B-K2 6
P-K5 QP×P 7 B-QN5ch B-Q2 8 P×KP N-N5 9 0-0 N-QB3 10 B×N B×B
11 Q×Qch R×Q 12 B-B4 0-0 13 P-KR3 B×N 14 P×B N-R3 15 B×N
P×B 16 N-K4 P-B4 17 P×Pe.p. B×P 18 N×P R-Q7 19 N×KP R-K1 20 N-
B5 R×QBP 21 N×P R-B2 22 N-Q6 R-KB1 23 QR-N1 B-K4 24 KR-Q1 R-
KN2ch 25 K-B1 R×P 26 N-B4 B-B3 27 R-Q6 B-R5 28 K-K2 R×BPch 39
K-K3 R-B7 30 K-Q4 R-QB2 31 R-N1ch K-B2 32 N-K3 R-Q7ch 33 K-K4
R×R 34 N-B5 R-B5ch 35 K-K5 R-K3ch 36 K-Q5 R-QN5 37 R-N7ch K-B3
38 R-N4 R×R 39 P×R R-K4ch 40 K-B4 R×N 41 P×R P-KR4 42 P-R4
K×P 43 P-R5 P-KR3 44 P-R6 B-B3 45 P-N4 P-R5 46 P-N5 P-R6 47 P-N6 P-
R7 48 P×P P-R8=Q 49 K-N3 P-R4 50 K-R4 Q-B3ch 51 K-R3 Q-R1 52 K-
N4 B-Q5 53 K-B4 K-K5 54 K-N5 P-R5 55 K-B4 P-R6 56 K-N3 P-R7 57 K-
B4 Q-Q4ch 58 K-N4 P-R8=Q 59 K-R3 Q-R8ch 60 K-N4 Q(R8)-R4mate.

White: BS 66/76
Black: CHUTE

Blackmar Gambit

1 P-Q4 P-Q4 2 P-K4 P×P 3 N-QB3 N-KB3 4 P-B3 P×P 5 Q×P Q×P 6 B-
K3 Q-QN5 7 0-0-0 B-N5 8 N-N5 N-R3 9 Q×P B×R 10 N-Q6ch Q×N 11 B-
QN5ch P-B3 12 B×Pch N-Q2 13 Q×Rch QN-N1 14 B-QN5 P-QR3 15
B×Nch K×B 16 Q-N7ch K-K3 18 Q-K4ch K-Q2 18 B-B4 P-K4 19 B×P Q-
R3ch 30 K×B B-Q3 21 N-B3 R-QB1 22 Q-N7ch B-B2 23 Q-Q5ch K-K1 24
B×B R×B 25 R-K1ch R-K2 26 R×Rch K×R 27 Q-K5ch Q-K3 28 Q×N
Q-Q4ch 29 K-B1 Q×P 30 Q-N7ch K-B3 31 Q-B6ch Q-K3 32 Q-B3ch K-N3
33 N-R4ch K-R4 34 Q-B3ch K×N 35 Q-B4ch K-R4 36 P-N4ch Q×P 37
Q×Pch K-R3 38 Q-B1 Q-N4ch 39 K-N1 Q-QR4 40 Q-R3 ch Q-R4 41 Q-
K6ch Q-N3 42 Q-K3ch Q-N4 43 Q-K6ch Q-B3 44 Q-R3ch K-N3 45 Q-N4ch
K-B2 46 Q-QB4ch K-N3 47 Q-K4ch K-R3 48 P-N4 Q-B8ch 49 K-R2 Q-B2ch
50 K-R3 Q-B3 51 Q-K3ch K-N3 52 Q-Q3ch K-R3 53 Q-R3ch K-N3 54 K-N3
Q-B2ch 55 K-R3 Q-QB5 56 Q-KN3ch K-B2 57 Q-KB3ch K-N3 58 Q-KN3ch
K-B2 Draw agreed.

Round 3

White: CHAOS
Black: KAISSA

King's Indian Defence

1 P-Q4 N-KB3 2 P-QB4 P-B4 3 P-Q5 P-Q3 4 N-QB3 P-KN3 5 P-K4 B-N2 6
B-K2 0-0 7 B-N5 P-KR3 8 B-K3 Q-N3 9 Q-Q2 N-N5 10 B×N B×B 11 P-B3

B-Q2 12 B×RP B×B 13 Q×B Q×P 14 R-N1 Q×Nch 15 Q-Q2 Q×Qch
16 K×Q B-B1 17 N-K2 K-N2 18 P-KR4 R-R1 19 N-B4 N-Q2 20 P-R5 P-
KN4 21 N-Q3 R-QN1 22 P-B4 N-B3 23 P-K5 N-K5ch 24 K-K3 N-N6 25 R-
R2 P×Pch 26 K×P N×Pch 27 K-B3 B-B4 28 R-Q1 B×N 29 R×B P×P 30
R-KR3 N-B3 31 R-KN3ch K-B1 32 R-K3 P-N4 33 R×P P×P 34 R-B5 P-B6
35 P-Q6 P×P 36 K-K3 R-K1ch 37 K-Q3 P-B5ch 38 K×P(B4) R-B1ch 39 K-
N3 P-B7 40 R×K P-B8=Q 41 R(N3)-KB3 R-QN1ch 42 K-R4 Q-QB5ch 43
K-R5 Q-N4 mate.

White: CHESS 4.6
Black: DUCHESS
Petroff Defence
1 P-K4 P-K4 2 N-KB3 N-KB3 3 P-Q4 P×P 4 P-K5 N-K5 5 Q×P P-Q4 6
P×Pe.p N×QP 7 B-Q3 N-B3 8 Q-KB4 P-KN3 9 0-0 B-N2 10 B-Q2 Q-B3 11
Q×Q B×Q 12 N-B3 0-0 13 N-Q5 B×P 14 QR-N1 B-N2 15 N×P R-N1 16
B-KB4 R-Q1 17 N-QN5 B-B1 18 B-N5 R-Q2 19 KR-K1 P-N3 20 N-B3 P-B4
21 N-Q5 K-R1 22 B-KB4 B-QN2 23 N-N5 R-B1 24 N-B6 R(Q2)-QB2 25 N-
K6 R-B2 26 N×B R(B2)×N(B1) 27 N×P K×N 28 B×N R(B1)-Q1 29 B-
KB4 R-Q5 30 B-KN5 R-KN5 31 P-KB4 N-QR4 32 R-K7ch K-N1 33 P-N3
K-B1 34 R(N1)-K1 B-B6 35 B-KR6ch K-N1 36 R(K1)-K3 B-B5 37 B×B
P×B 38 P-KR3 R×KBP 39 B×R R×P 40 R(K3)×P R-QN7 41 R-K8ch
K-B2 42 R(K4)-K7ch K-B3 43 B-K5ch K-N4 44 B×R N-B5 45 B-Blch K-B3
46 R-K6ch K-N2 47 B-N5 N-Q3 48 R×N K-B2 49 R-K7ch K-N1 50 R-
Q8mate.

White: ELSA
Black: MASTER
Pirc Defence
1 P-K4 P-Q3 2 P-Q4 N-KB3 3 N-QB3 P-KN3 4 N-B3 B-N2 5 B-K2 0-0 6 0-0
P-N3 7 B-KN5 B-N2 8 P-K5 N-K5 9 N×N B×N 10 B-Q3 B-N2 11 Q-K2
P×P 12 P×P P-KB3 13 B-QB4ch K-R1 14 QR-Q1 Q-B1 15 B-R4 Q-N5 16
P-KR3 Q-R4 17 P-KN4 Q-R3 18 R-Q3 P×P 19 B×P Q×P 20 B×R
Q×Pch 21 K-R1 Q×B 22 B×Bch K×B 34 Q×Pch K-R3 24 Q-K3ch K-N2
25 Q-K7ch Q-B2 26 Q-K5ch Q-B3 27 Q×Pch Q-B2 28 Q-K5ch Q-B3 29
Q×Qch K×Q 30 R(B1)-Q1 P-KR4 31 P-B4 P-KN4 32 P-R4 P-N5 33 R-
Q6ch K-K2 34 K-N1 B×N 35 R(Q1)-Q2 P-R5 36 P-R5 N-B3 37 P×P P×P
38 R-Q7ch K-B1 39 R-Q1 B×R 40 R×B N-K4 41 P-N3 N-B6ch 42 K-N2 K-
K2 43 R-QN1 R-R7 44 R-QB1 R-N7 45 R-B3 K-B3 46 R-B1 R×NP 47 P-
B5 P×P 48 R×P R-N8 498 R-B5ch K-K3 50 R×N P×Rch 51 K×P R-N8
52 K-K4 P-R6 53 P-B4 R-KB8 54 K-Q4 P-R7 55 K-Q3 P-R7=Q 56 P-B5ch
K×P 57 Q4 R-B8 58 K-Q3 Q-K8 59 K-Q4 Q-K5mate.

White: OSTRICH
Black: BLACK KNIGHT

Sicilian Defence

1 P-K4 P-QB4 2 N-KB3 N-QB3 3 B-B4 N-B3 4 N-B3 N×P 5 B×Pch K×B
6 N×N P-Q4 7 N×P P-K4 8 N-B3 B-KB4 9 0-0 B-K2 10 P-Q3 P-Q5 11 R-
K1 Q-B2 12 Q-K2 B-Q3 13 B-Q2 Q-N3 14 P-B3 KR-K1 15 P×P P×P
White resigns. OSTRICH's computer broke down—(blew a fuse).

White: CHUTE
Black: BLITZ V

Petroff Defence

1 P-K4 P-K4 2 N-KB3 N-KB3 3 N×P P-Q3 4 N-KB3 N×P 5 Q-K2 Q-K2 6
P-Q3 N-KB3 7 Q×Qch B×Q 8 N-R3 B-N5 9 P-R3 B×N 10 P×B 0-0 11 N-
N5 N-R3 12 B-K3 P-B3 13 N×RP N-B4 14 B×N P×B 15 N×P P×N 16 P-
QR4 QR-K1 17 0-0-0 B-Q3 18 P-N3 R-K4 19 K-N1 R(B1)-K1 20 K-N2 P-R3
21 R-KN1 R-K8 22 R×R R×R 23 P-B3 B-R7 24 R-R1 B-K4 25 K-B2 N-Q4
26 P-QB4 N-N5ch 27 K-Q2 R-N8 28 K-K3 R×P 29 K-K4 B-Q5 30 R-R2 R-
R6 31 R-N2 R-R8 32 B-K2 R-K8 33 P-B4 R×Bch 34 K-B3 R-Q7 35 P-R5
N×P 36 R-N3 R×Pch 37 K-K4 N-N7 38 R-N3 N×P 39 R-N8ch K-R2 40 P-
R6 R×Pch 41 K×R B-K4ch 42 K-B5 B×R 43 K-K4 N-Q3ch 44 K-K3 P-B4
45 P-R4 P-N4 46 P×P P×P 47 K-K2 P-N5 48 K-K3 P-QB5 49 K-Q4 P-N6
50 K-K3 P-B6 51 K-Q3 P-N7 52 P-R7 B×P 53 K×P P-N8=Q 54 K-N3 Q-
N8ch 55 K-R4 Q-N7 56 K-R5 Q-R6mate.

White: TELL
Black: BCP

Two Knights Defence

1 P-K4 P-K4 2 N-KB3 3 N-QB3 B-B4 N-B3 4 N-B3 B-K2 5 0-0 0-0 6 B-Q5
P-Q3 7 B×N P×B 8 P-Q4 B-N5 9 P×P B×N 10 Q×B P×P 11 R-Q1 B-
Q3 12 B-K3 P-QR4 13 B-B5 Q-N1 14 B×B P×B 15 QR-N1 P-R5 16 P-
QN4 R-B1 17 Q-B5 R-Q1 18 P-N5 P×P 19 R×NP Q-B1 20 Q×Q KR×R
21 R-Q3 R-R3 22 R-N4 P-R6 23 R-N7 P-R3 24 P-B3 R(R3)-B3 25 N-Q5
N×N 26 P×N R-R3 27 R-Q2 R-R5 28 P-N4 P-K5 29 P×P R×KP 30 P-R3
R-K8ch 31 K-N2 R-QR8 32 R-B2 R×RP 33 R(N7)×P R(R7)×P 34
R(B7)-B3 R×Rch 35 R×R P-N4 36 R-B6 P-R7 37 R-N6ch K-B2 38 R-
N7ch K×R 39 P-R4 P×P 40 K-R3 P-R8=Q 41 K-N2 Q-Q5 42 K-R3
Q×QP 43 K-R2 R-B7ch 44 K-R3 Q-R8mate.

White: WITA
Black: BS 66/76

Albin Counter Gambit

1 P-Q4 P-Q4 2 P-QB4 P-K4 3 QP×P P-Q5 4 P-K4 P-KB4 5 B-Q3 N-QB3 6

N-KB3 B-N5ch 7 K-K2 P×P 8 B×P B-N5 9 Q-R4 P-Q6ch 10 K-B1 Q-Q2 11 B×N Q×B 12 Q×B B×N 13 P×B Q×KBP 14 R-N1 P-Q7 15 B×P Q-Q8ch 16 B-K1 Q-Q6ch 17 K-N2 Q-N3ch 18 K-R1 Q-K5ch 19 R-N2 P-QR4 20 Q-B3 Q-B4 21 R×P 0-0-0 22 Q×P Q-K5ch 23 P-B3 Q×KBPch 24 K-N1 Q-K6ch 25 K-R1 Q-K5ch 26 K-N1 Q-K6ch 27 K-R1 Q-K6ch 28 K-N1 Q-K6ch Draw by repetition.

White: BELLE
Black: DARK HORSE
Alekhine Defence
1 P-K4 N-KB3 2 P-K5 N-Q4 3 P-Q4 P-K3 4 B-Q3 N-QB3 5 N-KB3 B-K2 6 0-0 0-0 7 P-B3 P-Q3 8 R-K1 P×P 9 P×P P-QN3 10 Q-B2 P-N3 11 B-KR6 N(Q4)-N5 12 P×N N×NP 13 Q-N3 N×B 14 B×R B×B 15 R-Q1 B-QR3 16 N-K1 N×N 17 R×Q R×R 18 Q-R4 P-QN4 19 Q×B N-B7 20 N-B3 N×R 21 Q×NP R-Q7 22 Q-B1 N-B7 23 Q-B1 B-R3 24 N-K4 R-Q4 25 N-B6ch K-N2 26 Q×N R×P 27 N-K8ch K-B1 28 Q-B3 R-Q4 29 Q-R8ch K-K2 30 P-KN3 P-QB3 31 N-B6 R-Q8ch 32 K-N2 B-N4 33 N×P B-R3 34 Q-QN8 B-N2 35 Q×Pch R-Q2 36 Q-B5ch R-Q3 37 Q-KN5ch K-Q2 38 N-B6ch B×N 39 Q×B K-K1 40 P-QR4 R-Q4 41 Q-QB3 P-QB4 42 P0R5 R-B4 43 P-R6 P-B3 44 P-R7 R-Q4 45 P-R8=Qch K-K2 46 Q-N7ch R-Q2 47 Q×QBPch K-K1 48 Q(N7)-B8ch R-Q1 49 Q×Pmate.

Round 4

White: MASTER
Black: DUCHESS
Reti Opening
1 N-KB3 N-KB3 2 P-B4 P-Q4 3 P×P N×P 4 P-KN3 P-QB3 5 B-N2 P-K3 6 0-0 B-K2 7 P-Q4 0-0 8 P-K4 N-B3 9 N-B3 P-QN3 10 N-K5 B-R3 11 R-K1 Q-B1 12 B-K3 QN-Q2 13 N×N Q×N 14 P-K5 N-Q4 15 Q-R4 B-QN4 16 N×B P×N 17 Q QN3 KR-Q1 18 B-Q2 QR-B1 19 QR-B1 P-QR4 20 R×R R×R 21 R-QB1 R×Rch 22 B×R P-R5 23 Q-Q1 N-N5 24 B-K3 N×P 25 P-Q5 P×P 26 Q×QP Q×Q 27 B×Q N-N5 28 B-K4 B-B4 29 K-N2 B×B 30 P×B P-R3 31 K-B3 K-B1 32 P-R4 K-K2 33 P-R5 K-K3 34 K-B4 N-Q4ch 35 B×Nch K×B 36 P-KN4 P-KN5 37 K-B5 P-R6 38 P-K4ch K-B4 39 P×P P×P 40 P-K6 P×Pch 41 K-K5 P-R7 42 K×P P-R8=Q 43 P-N5 P×P 44 P-K5 Q-Q5 45 K-B5 Q-KB5ch 46 K-K6 P-N5 47 K-K7 P-N6 White resigns.

White: BS 66/76
Black: ELSA
King's Indian Defence
1 P-Q4 N-KB3 2 P-QB4 P-KN3 3 N-KB3 B-N2 4 N-B3 0-0 5 B-B4 N-R4 6 P-

K3 N×B 7 P×N P-QB4 8 P×P B×Nch 9 P×B Q-B2 10 Q-Q4 N-R3 11 P-B6 QP×P 12 P-KR3 R-Q1 13 Q-K3 Q-Q3 14 Q-K5 B-B4 15 P-N4 B-K3 16 P-N5 N-B4 17 R-QN1 Q-Q6 18 B×Q N×Bch 19 K-K2 N×Q 20 N×N P-B3 21 N×NP B×BPch 22 K-K3 P×N 23 P×P P×P 24 R×P R-Q6ch 25 K-K2 R-K1ch 26 R-K7 R×Rch 27 K-B1 R-N6mate.

White: BCP
Black: OSTRICH
Bishop's Opening
1 P-K4 P-K4 2 B-B4 N-KB3 3 P-Q4 P-Q3 4 N-KB3 B-N5 5 P×P B×N 6 P×B P×P 7 B×Pch K-K2 8 Q×Qch K×Q 9 0-0 QN-Q2 10 B-N5 P-KR3 11 B×Nch N×B 12 N-B3 B-N5 13 N-Q5 N×N 14 B×N P-B3 15 B-K6 K-K1 16 P-QR3 B-K2 17 KR-Q1 R-Q1 18 R×Rch B×R 19 R-Q1 R-B1 20 K-N2 B-N3 21 B-B5 R-B3 22 B-B8 R-B2 23 B-B5 K-B1 24 R-Q7 R×R 25 B×R B-Q5 26 P-B3 B-B4 27 P-N4 B-Q3 28 P-QB4 P-B4 29 P-N5 K-K2 30 B-B5 K-B3 31 P-KR4 P-KN3 32 B-Q7 P-KR4 33 P-R4 P-N4 34 P×Pch K×P 35 P-R5 P-R5 36 P-N6 P×P 37 P×P B-K2 38 B-K6 B-Q1 39 B-Q5 K-B5 40 B×P P-R6ch 41 K×P K×P 42 B-Q5 B×P 43 K-R2 K×P 44 K-R3 K-B6 45 K-R2 B-Q1 46 K-R3 B-N4 47 K-R2 B-B5ch 48 K-R3 B-N6 49 B-B6 B-K8 50 B-Q5 Draw agreed.

White: BLITZ V
Black: CHAOS
Sicilian Defence
1 P-K4 P-QB4 2 N-KB3 N-QB3 3 P-Q4 P×P 4 N×P N-B3 5 N-QB3 P-K3 6 B-K2 B-N5 7 0-0 B×N 8 P×B N×P 9 N×N QP×N 10 Q×Qch K×Q 11 B-Q3 N-B4 12 B-K3 N×B 13 KR-Q1 P-K4 14 P×N K-B2 15 QR-N1 B-B4 16 R-N3 P-QN3 17 R-Q2 P-B3 18 P-KR3 QR-Q1 19 P-Q4 K-B1 20 P×P R×R 21 B×R P×P 22 B-N5 P-KR3 23 B-R4 P-QN4 24 P-R3 P-QR4 25 P-B3 K-Q2 26 K-R2 K-K3 27 R-N2 R-KB1 28 R-K2 B-Q6 29 R-Q2 B-B8 30 K-N1 B-B5 31 B-Q8 P-R5 32 B-B7 K-B4 33 P-N4ch K-N4 34 B×P R×P 35 R-Q6 B-Q4 36 K-R2 K-R5 37 B×P R×RPch 38 K-N1 P-R4 39 B-K5 K×P 40 B-Q4 R-N6ch 41 K-B2 P-R5 42 R-N6h K-B5 43 R-R6 R-N7ch 44 K-B1 K-N6 45 R-N6ch K-R6 46 R-Q6 B-B5ch 47 K-K1 R-K7ch 48 K-Q1 R-K3 49 R-Q7 K-R7 50 K-Q2 R-K7ch 51 K-Q1 P-R6 52 R-Q6 R-K3 53 R-Q7 B-N6ch 54 K-Q2 K-R8 55 B-K3 B-B7 56 K×B R×B 57 R-Q6 K-N7 58 R×P P-R7 59 R-KN6ch R-N6 60 R-KR6 P-R8=Q 61 R×Q K×R 62 K-Q2 K-N8 63 K-B2 R-N5 64 K-Q2 K-B8 65 K-Q1 R-QB5 66 K-Q2 K-B7 67 K-Q3 K-K8 68 K-B2 K-K7 69 K-N2 K-Q7 70 K-N1 K×P 71 K×B1 R-B3 72 K-Q1 R-K3 73 K-B1 R-K8mate.

White: TELL
Black: CHUTE

Sicilian Defence

1 P-K4 P-QB4 2 B-B4 P-Q3 3 Q-R5 P-K3 4 B-N5ch N-Q2 5 N-QB3 KN-B3 6 Q-R4 P-QR3 7 B-K2 P-Q4 8 P×P P×P 9 N-B3 P-QN4 10 N×QP N×N 11 Q-K4ch B-K2 12 Q×N N-N3 13 Q-B6ch B-Q2 14 Q-K4 0-0 15 0-0 P-B4 16 Q-K5 R-B3˙17 B-Q3 B-Q3 18 Q-B3 N-Q4 19 Q-N3 P-QB5 20 B×QBP P×B 21 Q×P B-K3 22 N-N5 R-R3 23 P-KR4 N-K6 24 N×B B-R7ch 25 K-R1 N×Q 26 N×Q R×P 27 N-K6 B-B5ch 28 K-N1 B-R7ch 29 K-R1 B-K4ch 30 K-N1 R-K1 31 N-B5 B-R7ch 32 K-R1 B-Q3ch 33 K-N1 B×N 34 P-Q3 N-K4 35 B-N5 R-KN5 36 B-B1 N-B6ch 37 K-R1 R-KR5 mate.

White: BELLE
Black: CHESS 4.6

French Defence

1 P-K4 N-QB3 2 N-KB3 P-K3 3 P-Q4 P-Q4 4 N-B3 B-N5 5 P-K5 KN-K2 6 P-QR3 B×Nch 7 P×B N-R4 8 B-QN5ch B-Q2 9 B-Q3 R-QB1 10 N-N5 P-KR3 11 N-B3 P-QB4 12 P×P R×P 13 B-K3 R×P 14 B×QRP N-B5 15 0-0 R×RP 16 R×R N×R 17 B-QB5 Q-R4 18 B-Q6 N-B5 19 Q-R1 N-B3 20 Q×Q N(B3)×Q 21 R-R1 B-B1 22 P-B3 N-B3 23 R-R4 N×B 24 P×N K-Q2 25 R-KN4 P-KN4 26 B-B2 K×P 27 R-QR4 P-N4 28 R-R1 P-QN5 29 P×P N×P 30 B-N1 B-Q2 31 K-R1 P-B4 32 N-Q4 R-QB1 33 N-K2 B-N4 34 N-N1 R-B8 35 R-R5 R×B 36 P-B3 B-B8 37 P-R4 R-N7 38 P×P B×Pch 39 K-R2 P×P 40 R-R4 B×Pch 41 K-N3 B-R4 42 K-R3 P-B5 43 R-R8 B-N3 44 K-N4 R-N7ch 45 K-R3 R×N 46 K-R2 R-N5 47 R-Q8ch K-K4 48 R-KN8 B-K5 49 R-N7 B-B6 50 R-KR7 N-Q6 51 R-R3 R-N7ch 52 K-R1 N-B7mate.

White: WITA
Black: DARK HORSE

English Opening

1 P-QB4 N-QB3 2 P-KN3 P-K4 3 B-N2 Q-B3 4 N-QB3 B-B4 5 N-B3 P-Q3 6 P-Q3 Q-Q1 7 B-K3 B×B 8 P×B N-B3 9 0-0 B-K3 10 N-KN5 K-Q2 11 Q-R4 P-QR4 12 Q-N5 R-QN1 13 N-R4 P-KN3 14 P-QR3 R-K1 15 QR-B1 P-R3 16 N×B P×N 17 N-B3 Q-K2 18 P-R3 P-N4 19 P-N3 P-N5 20 P-Q4 P×RP 21 B×P Q-N2 22 K-R1 Q×P 23 R-B3 Q-N3 24 R-KN1 Q-B7 25 R×N Q×N 26 P-Q5 Q×KP 27 P×Nch K-Q1 28 B-N4 Q-N4 29 R-B2 P-N3 30 B-R3 Q-K6 31 R-B3 Q×KP 32 R-B6 Q-K5ch 33 K-R2 Q-B7ch 34 R-N2 Q-K5 35 R×KP Q-B5ch 36 K-R1 Q-KB8ch 37 K-R2 R×R 38 R-N8ch K-K2 39 B×R Q-B7ch 40 K-R3 Q-B6ch 41 K-R2 Q-R4ch 42 K-N3 R×Rch 43 B×R Q-N4ch 44 K-B2 Q×B 45 P-N4 46 P×P Q-KB1ch 47 K-N2 K-Q1 48 Q-Q5 P-R4 49 P-N5 P-R5 50 K-R3 Q-R3 51 Q-N8ch K-K2 52 Q-N8 Q-K6ch Draw agreed.

White: BLACK KNIGHT
Black: KAISSA

Centre Counter

1 P-K4 P-Q4 2 P×P N-KB3 3 P-Q4 N×P 4 P-QB4 N-N3 5 N-KB3 P-N3 6
N-B3 B-N2 7 P-KR3 0-0 8 B-K3 N-B3 9 Q-Q2 P-K4 10 P-Q5 N-K2 11 P-
KN4 P-KB4 12 0-0-0 P-K5 13 N-R2 B-Q2 14 B-K2 B-R5 15 N×B N×N 16
B-Q4 B×B 17 Q×B Q-Q3 18 R-Q2 P-B4 19 Q-K3 QR-K1 20 Q-N5 P×P
21 P×P R×P 22 B-Q1 R×R 23 B×N R×N 24 R×R Q×R 25 B×R Q-
N8ch 26 K-B2 Q-N7ch 27 Q-Q2 Q×P 28 Q-B2 N-B4 29 Q×P Q-N7ch 30
K-N3 Q-N6ch 31 K-R4 P-QR3 32 Q-QB8 N-Q3 33 Q-K6ch K-B1 34 B-Q7
Q-B5 35 P-B5 P-K6ch 36 K-R3 N-B5ch 37 K-N3 N-R4ch 38 K-R3 N-B5ch
39 K-N3 N-K4 40 Q-K8ch K-N2 41 Q-K7ch K-R3 42 Q-K6 Q-B5ch 43 K-R3
Q×BPch 44 K-N3 Q-B5ch 45 K-R3 Q-Q6ch 46 P-N3 N-B5ch 47 K-N4 P-K7
48 K-B5 N-Q3 49 K-N6 N-K5 50 K×P N-B4ch 51 K-N6 N×Q 52 P×N P-
K8=Q 53 K-N7 Q-R4 54 P-N4 Q(Q6)-Q4ch 55 B-B6 Q(R4)×NPch 56 K-
B7 Q(Q4)-Q3ch 57 K-B8 Q(N5)-N1mate.

Bibliography

Chess and Computers (1976), Levy D., (Computer Science Press, Potomac, Maryland) contains an extensive bibliography of English and Russian language publications on our subject. Since the time of publication of that work many new publications have appeared and we list a number of them below. We have separated them into three categories - books, papers of general interest and technical articles.

Books

Advances in Computer Chess (1977), Clark, M. (Ed.), University of Edinburgh Press.

Chess Skill in Man and Machine (1977), Frey, P.W. (Ed.), Springer-Verlag, New York.

The World Computer Chess Championship (1976), Hayes J. and Levy, D., University of Edinburgh Press.

1974 U.S. Computer Chess Championship (1976), Levy, D., Computer Science Press, Potomac, Maryland.

1976 U.S. Computer Chess Championship (1977), Levy, D., Computer Science Press, Potomac, Maryland.

General Interest

Benko, P. (1978). "The "Amateur" World Champion: An interview with Max Euwe," *Chess Life and Review* 33, 410-413.

Berliner, H. (1976). "Outstanding performances by CHESS 4.5 against human competition." *SIGART Newsletter,* No. 60, 12-13.

Berliner, H. (1977). "Two games from the Minnesota Open." *SIGART Newsletter,* No. 62, 9-10.

Berliner, H. (1977). "CHESS 4.5 vs. Levy." *SIGART Newsletter* No. 62, 11.

Berliner, H. (1978). "A chronology of computer chess and its literature." *Artificial Intelligence* 10, 201-214.

Byrne, R. (1978). "Fischer vs. the computer." *The New York Times.* July 30, 30.

Cahlander, D. (1977). "The computer is a fish, or is it?" *SIGART Newsletter, No. 62, 8-9.* Douglas, J.R. (1978). "GM Walter Browne vs. CHESS 4.6" *Chess Life and Review* 33, 363-364.

"First microcomputer chess tournament." (1978). *Chess Life and Review* 33, 311.

Goldwater, W. (1977). "My game and animadversions." *Chess Life and Review* 32, 313-314.

Kaplan, J. (1977). "Let's go, big beige machine!" *Sports Illustrated,* August 22, 42.

Lasker, Edward. (1977). "But will it fly?" *Chess Life and Review* 32, 314.

Levy, D. (1977a). "Invasion from cyberland." *Chess Life and Review* 32, 312-313.

Marsland, T.A. (1976). "1976 Canadian computer-chess workshop." *SIGART Newsletter, No. 60, 22.*

Marsland, T.A. (1977). "A comprehensive list of computer chess literature." Tech. Report TR77-4, Dept. of Comput. Sci., Univ. of Alberta.

Michie, D. (1977). "David Levy challenge game, 1 April 1977." *SIGART Newsletter,* No. 62, 10-11.

Morrison, M.E. (1976). "4th Annual Paul Masson American Class Championship," *Chess Life and Review* 31, 553.

Newborn, M.M. (1978). "Computer chess: recent progress and future expectations." *Proc. Jerusalem Conf. on Inf. Tech.*

Richter, H. (1976). "The first German computer chess championship at Dortmund." *SIGART Newsletter,* No. 56, 2.

Soule, S. and Marsland, T.A. (1975). "Canadian computer chess tournament." *SIGART Newsletter,* No. 54, 12-13.

Technical Articles

Adelson-Velskiy, G.M., Arlazarov, V.L., and Donskoy, M.V. (1975). "Some methods of controlling the tree search in chess programs." *Artificial Intelligence* 6, 361-371.

Akl, S. and Newborn, M.M. (1977). "The principal continuation and the killer heuristic." *Proc. 1977 Annual Conf. of the Asoc. Comput. Mach.* 466-473.

Arlazarov, V.L. and Futer, A.V. (1978). "Computer analysis of a Rook end-game", *Machine Intelligence* 9 (J.E. Hayes, D. Michie, and L.I. Milulich, eds.) University of Edinburgh Press (in press).

Baudet, G.M. (1978). "On the branching factor of the alpha-beta pruning algorihm." *Artificial Intelligence* 9, 177-199.

Berliner, H. (1975). "A new subfield of computer chess," *SIGART Newsletter,* No. 53, 20-21.

Griffith, A.K. (1976). "Empirical exploration of the performance of the alpha-beta tree search heuristic." *IEEE Trans. on Computers,* 6-10.

Knuth, D.E., and Moore, R.N. (1975). "An analysis of alpha-beta pruning," *Artificial Intelligence* 6, 293-326.

Michalski, R. and Negri, P. (1975). "An experiment on inductive learning in chess endgames: the King-Pawn case." *NATO Adv. Study Inst. on Machine Repres. of Knowledge,* Santa Cruz.

Michie, D. (1976). "An advice taking system for computer chess." *Computer Bulletin,* December 12-14.

Michie, D., and Bratko, I., (1978). "Advice tables representations of chess end-game knowledge." *Proc. AISB Summer Conference,* Hamburg.

Newborn, M.M. (1977). "The efficiency of the alpha-beta search on trees with branch-dependent terminal node scores," *Artificial Intelligence 8,* 137-153.

Slate, D. and Mittman, B. (1978). "CHESS 4.6 - Where do we go from here?" *Proc. Jerusalem on Information Tech.* 84-88.

CHESS NOTES